THOMAS MERTON
—Evil and Why We Suffer

THOMAS MERTON
— *Evil and Why We Suffer*

From Purified Soul Theodicy to Zen

David E. Orberson

CASCADE *Books* • Eugene, Oregon

THOMAS MERTON—EVIL AND WHY WE SUFFER
From Purified Soul Theodicy to Zen

Cascade Books
An Imprint of Wipf and Stock Publishers
199 W. 8th Ave., Suite 3
Eugene, OR 97401

www.wipfandstock.com

PAPERBACK ISBN: 978-1-5326-3899-2
HARDCOVER ISBN: 978-1-5326-3900-5
EBOOK ISBN: 978-1-5326-3901-2

Cataloging-in-Publication data:

Names: Orberson, David E., author.
Title: Thomas Merton—evil and why we suffer : from purified soul theodicy to Zen /
    David E. Orberson.
Description: Eugene, OR: Cascade Books, 2018. | Includes bibliographical references
    and index.
Identifiers: ISBN: 978-1-5326-3899-2 (paperback). | ISBN: 978-1-5326-3900-5
    (hardcover). | ISBN: 978-1-5326-3901-2 (epub).
Subjects: LCSH: Merton, Thomas, 1915–1968—Criticism and interpretation. |
    Theodicy. | Good and evil. | Religion—Philosophy.
Classification: BX4705.M542 O75 2018 (print). | BX4705 (ebook).

Manufactured in the U.S.A.

Transcript of unpublished recording of Thomas Merton used with Permission of the
Merton Legacy Trust and the Thomas Merton Center at Bellarmine University.

To Olivia and Beth

Contents

Acknowledgments

I had a great deal of support and guidance throughout this project. Special thanks to Patrick Pranke, Annette Allen, J. Milburn Thompson, and Thomas Maloney for their insights and encouragement throughout the formative stage of this project. I am also grateful to Dr. Paul Pearson, Director and Archivist at the Thomas Merton Center, for his help and feedback from the inception of this idea to its publication. He and Assistant Director Mark Meade both gave generously of their time and made every one of the center's vast resources available.

On a personal note, I could have never completed this book were it not for my wonderful family. My parents and brother have given me a lifetime of unconditional love and encouragement. Finally, my wife, Beth, and daughter, Olivia, have my eternal love and gratitude for their tireless patience and support, and most of all for reminding me what's most important in life.

Preface

Thomas Merton was one of the most prolific and important Catholic writers of the twentieth century. He authored over sixty books, scores of essays and articles, and hundreds of poems addressing a wide variety of subjects. His autobiography was an international best seller, and many of his writings helped shape the conversation about a host of spiritual and social issues. Merton wrote about many topics that one might expect a monk to address: e.g., the importance of contemplation, prayer, the state of the Catholic Church and monasticism, and the like. However, while cloistered and living apart from the world in rural Kentucky, Merton was still very much a part of it, through his writing and correspondence. In fact, Merton wrote a great deal about the social ills of the day: racism, nuclear proliferation, and the ways technology can alienate humanity. Finally, during the last years of his life Merton wrote about his exploration of Zen and Buddhism and thus helped establish an important bridge for the Western Christian exploration of Eastern thought.

Several aspects of Merton's life make him a fascinating figure to study. He had the ability to convey insights about the human experience and about God that resonate with readers. As one biographer wrote,

> He had the ability to articulate, often with brilliance and astounding perceptiveness, the vagaries of the human condition: hope vying with despair, love with hatred, communion with alienation. He could reach deep into the human heart and surface questions for his readers that, till they read him, lay hidden and unasked, struggling for expression. Unique synthesizer that he was, he could put things together that no one had seen as one before. He knew how to raise to a new level of understanding people's perception of God and prayer and human life. He was able to show that life was for

the living in that in this living we find God and self and meaning
and purpose.[1]

As I mentioned above, Merton wrote about more than just spiritual
matters. He was on the forefront in speaking out against the war in Vietnam, the nuclear arms race, racism, and other social ills of that time. One
friend described it this way:

> He was as capacious a mind as I've ever encountered. He took ev-
> erything in, tied it together, and somehow it came out always in an
> orderly way. It was a good thing that he chose the essay as his way
> of dealing with the world. He was a monk and he just had little
> hunks of time to write. But in two or three hours it's amazing the
> cogent gems he could turn out. He was an exceptionally sensitive
> man, as well as an exceptionally religious man. The race situation,
> the bomb—he saw the consequences clearly and early, and from a
> place so far out of the mainstream. He was years ahead of almost
> everybody in his concern that the machines were going to take
> over—the whole business of dehumanization. And he was quite
> right.[2]

While many are drawn to the perspicacity of Merton's writings, no
one familiar with his life story would confuse him for being any kind of, to
use one of his own terms, a pseudoangel. He never claimed to be a saint,
and was thoroughly human, filled with the same conflicting and competing
instincts that live in all of us. Merton's life as a cloistered monk did not
shield him from conflict, worry, or self-doubt. In fact, many biographers
point to the fact that Merton was restless. Once he attained one thing, he
wanted another. As one friend of his put it:

> He loved people, he really loved people. But at the same time as he
> loved them he wanted his distance from them. People would often
> say to me that they found it odd, if not slightly scandalous, that a
> monk could share a few beers with you, just call from the monas-
> tery and arrange for a picnic, and yet I think this was a lifeline for
> him. He didn't want the secular life but he needed the reassurance
> that came by being with people. He was a fusser and a complainer
> to tell you the truth and when you read his journals you see that
> when he is here he wants to be there: if he's in the hermitage, he
> needs to get out; if he is following one diet maybe he should be

---

1. Shannon, *Silent Lamp*, 5–6.
2. Wilkes, *Merton, by Those Who Knew Him Best*, 88.

really following another. He was, with all these contradictions, just plain human.[3]

Scholars began writing about Merton while he was still alive. Since his death in 1968, hundreds of books and countless articles have been written about various aspects of work. However, one fascinating area that has not been adequately explored concerns the problem of evil. That is, how did he affirm a belief in an all-loving and all-powerful God in light of evil and suffering in the world?

Merton never wrote a book or even an article dedicated to the problem of evil. Because of this it is necessary to examine each instance where he does address this topic throughout his entire canon—i.e., books, journals, correspondence, articles, and talks he gave to novice monks, letting him speak for himself. In this way one can discover his theodicy, that is, his justification for belief in a God who is all-loving and all-powerful, in spite of the evil and suffering in the world. I follow this thread of thought throughout Merton's life. I argue that Merton did indeed espouse a particular kind of theodicy. Specifically, for most of his adult life Merton believed that suffering leads to the purification of the human soul. In addition, he often states that God causes this suffering in order to bring about a good. Thus, I have dubbed this response to the problem of evil as a Purified Soul Theodicy. As will be shown, Merton also believed that God does not abandon us to suffer alone. God is always with us, even when and especially when we suffer. Merton consistently puts forth this belief in a variety of writings over decades. However, his attitude toward the problem of evil began to change in his last few years of his life. Remarks he gave to two different religious groups offer an interesting contrast to demonstrate this change. First, in late November 1963 Merton was serving as master of novices, instructing new monks that had joined the order. After the death of President Kennedy, he gave these new monks the latest news about the assassination. Without hesitation, he told the group that this act, while tragic, was the will of God. When challenged by a novice on this point, he unwaveringly continued, discussing the uncanny nature of Oswald's shot being able to find its target, and declaring that such acts were part of an elaborate operation of cause and effect. However, just five years later, remarks he gave to a group of priests and nuns in Alaska are markedly different. In discussing the book of Job, and the problem of evil, his long held and espoused purified soul theodicy is nowhere to be found. In addition, in stark opposition to his comments to

3. Quoted in Higgins, *Thomas Merton*, 73–74.

the novice monks in 1963, Merton now rails against trying to understand God and the problem of evil through any kind of schematized system of causes and effects, in essence abandoning the task of theodicy altogether. What could have caused such a change? I argue that his immersion in Zen, primarily understood through the writings of D. T. Suzuki, significantly contributed to this transition.

In the following four chapters, bracketed by this brief introduction and a conclusion, I explore Merton's life, the concept of the problem of evil, Merton's own theodicy, and finally how and why he abandoned it. Chapter 1 focuses on Merton's life, with special attention on the theme of suffering throughout it. In chapter 2 I provide a survey of prominent contemporary theodicies so that Merton's can be properly contextualized. Next, in chapter 3 I begin the process of examining Merton's works to identify his own purified soul theodicy. Then, in chapter 4 I demonstrate how Merton's response to the problem of evil changed during the last years of his life, and argue that his increased immersion in Buddhism and Zen was a significant factor leading him to abandon the task of theodicy. Finally, in a brief conclusion I pull together ideas from these chapters and draw some overall conclusions.

1

The Life of Thomas Merton

Thomas Merton was a wonderfully kaleidoscopic figure. Many fine biographies[1] have been written in an attempt to convey a sense of the man. He was many things to different people: poet, spiritual writer, mystic, contemplative, priest and monk, peace activist, and interfaith pioneer. This chapter's goal is to provide a biographical sketch of the whole man, and given the greater scope of this book, to pay special attention to the theme of suffering in his life. To be clear at the outset, I do not believe that Merton was an especially tragic figure or deserves to be pitied. Instead, I pay particular attention to the personal suffering in his life so that readers can better appreciate the later study of his thoughts about God's role in human suffering. Here then is the extraordinary story of Thomas Merton.

Childhood

Thomas Merton was born during a snowstorm in Prades, France, on January 31, 1915. His parents had met in 1911 while enrolled as art students at the Tudor-Hart Academy in Paris. His father, Owen, was an artist and musician, and his mother, Ruth, was a dancer and painter.[2] Within a year

---

1. While there are many good biographies, Michael Mott's official one, *The Seven Mountains of Thomas Merton,* remains the most in-depth and comprehensive. I refer to it frequently throughout this chapter.

2. Mott, *Seven Mountains,* 5–6.

of Thomas's birth the family had moved to America to be near Ruth's family, and so that Owen could avoid conscription into the Great War. Ruth's parents, Samuel "Pop" and Martha "Bonnemaman" Jenkins would play an important role in Merton's upbringing. Owen and Ruth lead a largely hand-to-mouth existence while living in America. They had vowed not to accept any money from Ruth's parents, except when they needed medicine for young Thomas.[3] Owen was always able to keep the family afloat financially, if just barely, by working a series of odd jobs including as a church organist, as a piano player at a local theater, and as a landscaper.[4]

Young Thomas was observed to be a bright and curious child. His mother chronicled his every activity, even organizing these observations, and sending what she called Tom's Book to Owen's family in New Zealand. By all accounts Thomas was the center of his mother's world, but that dynamic changed in November 1918 with the birth of his brother, John Paul. Ruth could be cold, and was not reluctant to discipline a headstrong Thomas. In his autobiography Merton recounts a time that he was sent to bed early, "for stubbornly spelling 'which' without the first 'h': 'w-i-c-h.' I remember brooding about this as an injustice. 'What do they think I am, anyway?' After all, I was still only five years old."[5] However, as biographer Michael Mott points out, after the birth of his brother, "love, with both encouragement and correction, had been replaced by cold, intellectual criticism."[6]

Merton's young life was about to face a major crisis when his mother discovered she had stomach cancer. He never knew exactly how long she struggled with her diagnosis while still living at home, but when she was finally admitted to a nearby hospital, the family moved in with Ruth's parents in Douglaston, New York. Thomas would never see his mother again. He was not allowed to see his mother in the hospital, and, sadly, Merton always believed that this was at his mother's request. Although Merton knew his mother was sick in the hospital, the six-year-old was not aware how dire the situation actually was until his father handed him a letter from his mother. This note informed the young boy about the grim news. As Merton recalled,

> Then one day Father gave me a note to read. I was very surprised.
> It was for me personally, and it was in my mother's handwriting.

3. Ibid., 15–16.
4. Ibid., 16.
5. Merton, *Seven Storey Mountain*, 10.
6. Mott, *Seven Mountains*, 17.

I don't think she had ever written to me before—there had never been any occasion for it. Then I understood what was happening, although, as I remember, the language of the letter was confusing to me. Nevertheless, one thing was quite evident. My mother was informing me, by mail, that she was about to die, and would never see me again.[7]

Sadly, for the rest of his life Merton would think that his mother had decided to deliver this news in a letter rather than in person. It is now known that Bellevue Hospital had a policy that prevented children from visiting the general wards, and this was Ruth's only way to communicate with her son.[8] Ruth died October 3, 1921. Merton would reflect on this, and other early childhood memories, with the lingering belief that his mother was more cerebral, and less caring and loving, as a parent.[9]

Within a year of Ruth's death Owen decided he needed to make a change and rededicate himself to his painting. He made the decision to move to Bermuda, and took Thomas with him, leaving his other son, John Paul, in the care of Ruth's parents in New York. Thomas, now age seven, and his father left for Bermuda in the fall of 1922. While there, Owen met aspiring novelist Evelyn Scott. The two fell in love, despite the fact that Evelyn was married, and they had a tempestuous relationship. Young Thomas did not care for Evelyn at all, and was not bashful in voicing his displeasure to the couple. During this time Owen wrote to a friend stating that "Tom's jealousy and irreconcilableness are perfectly enormous."[10] It appears there was no love lost from Evelyn either. In fact, she confided to a friend that, "Tom is a morbid and possessive kid and Owen is made morbid about Tom through various things that occurred in connection with Ruth. Tom is, and will be until he is big enough to be set adrift a constant obstacle to piece [sic] of mind."[11] This period was made even more unsettling for Thomas by

---

7. Merton, *Seven Storey Mountain*, 14.

8. Horan, *Franciscan Heart*, 37.

9. In a letter to theologian Rosemary Radford Reuther, whom he had been quarreling with in previous correspondence, Merton wrote, "I promise I won't get up in the air again. I don't know why you frightened me so. ('Cerebral' probably because I resented my mother's intellectuality) (or what I later interpreted as that)." Merton, *Hidden Ground of Love*, 509.

10. Mott, *Seven Mountains*, 33.

11. Ibid., 24.

the fact that Owen would occasionally leave young Thomas with friends so that he could go on trips to sell his art.[12]

After a couple years in Bermuda, the father and son returned to America so that Owen could exhibit and sell some of his paintings. Flush with money, Owen made plans to return to France to resume his painting with old friends. This time, the eight-year-old Thomas would stay in America with his maternal grandparents, Pop and Bonnemaman. While he was happy to reunite with his grandparents and brother, he missed his father and felt abandoned during this time. Thomas was elated when in July 1925 his father returned to America to fetch him and take him back to France. Many years later Merton looked back at this, describing, "I realized today after mass what a desperate, despairing childhood I had. Around the age of 7-9-10, when mother was dead and father was in France and Algeria. How much it meant when he came to take me to France. It really saved me."[13] While Thomas was reunited with his father, his younger brother, John Paul, would once again stay in New York with their grandparents.

In August 1925 Owen and Thomas left for Saint-Antonin, France. Once they arrived and were settled, Thomas attended the Lycée Ingress in Montauban. He lived at the school and took a train on the weekends to spend one day a week with his father.[14] That first summer in France, Thomas faced his first major health crisis, being treated for what was believed to be tuberculosis.[15] Merton was miserable at the Lycée and in June 1928 his father came to take him out of the school. Merton described his joy and relief to leave: "I looked around me like a man that has had the chains struck from his hands. How the light sang on the brick walls of the prison whose gates had just burst open before me, sprung by some invisible and beneficent power: my escape from the Lycée was, I believe, providential."[16]

Thomas and his father continued to roam, and in 1929 moved to England. There Merton attended a boarding school in Oakham. Owen was still struggling financially, so Thomas's grandfather Pop once again stepped in to help his grandson by paying his tuition.[17] In the summer of 1930, Pop came to visit, and brought news that would have a significant impact on Merton's

12. Merton, *Seven Storey Mountain*, 19–20.

13. Merton, *Learning to Love*, 11–12.

14. Mott, *Seven Mountains*, 37.

15. Ibid., 37–38.

16. Merton, *Seven Storey Mountain*, 60.

17. Mott, *Seven Mountains*, 51.

life. During his stay, Pop took Thomas aside and informed him that he had made arrangements to financially provide for him and his brother, for the rest of their lives. Pop[18] had created a trust that contained a diversified portfolio of assets. Thomas and his brother John Paul would own shares of various stocks, as well as property on Long Island and in Coral Gables, Florida. In fact, the Merton brothers would even own an island, Stone Island, off Machiasport, Maine. Thomas would receive an allowance until he turned twenty-one, but Pop would not be administering the trust from New York. Instead, Thomas's godfather, Tom Bennett, would watch over his ward from his London home.[19]

Later in 1930, tragedy once again visited Merton's life when his father, Owen, was hospitalized for a brain tumor. In January 1931, one week after Thomas returned to school from Christmas break, his father passed away.[20] At the age of fifteen Thomas Merton was an orphan. Despite this setback, he excelled at school. He corresponded frequently with his grandparents in America and would spend summers with them.[21] At age seventeen Thomas faced another health crisis. This time, he became seriously ill after developing blood poisoning from an infected toe, actually coming close to death.[22]

The College Years

After successfully finishing school at Oakham, Merton was accepted into Clare College at Cambridge in 1933. His plan at that time was to complete his education and then enter the diplomatic corps. Unfortunately, his time at Cambridge would prove to be a disaster. Merton quickly took up with the wrong crowd, ignoring his studies and spending evenings in pubs.[23] At one point during his first semester his raucous behavior may have even included participation in a mock crucifixion.[24] After the first term, his

---

18. Samuel "Pop" Jenkins worked for a New York publisher but made his fortune by inventing a kind of picture book that would tell the story of a popular film using stills from the movie. Mott, *Seven Mountains*, 12.

19. Ibid., 53.

20. Ibid., 55.

21. During the even years the family would come to Thomas, and he would go to New York on the odd numbered years (ibid., 63).

22. Ibid., 62.

23. Mott, *Seven Mountains*, 75.

24. Ibid., 78–79.

godfather and trust administrator, Tom Bennett, called Thomas to London for a stern lecture. Bennet read Merton the riot act for his poor academic performance and took him to task for racking up debts for tailored clothing, books, alcohol and trips to nightclubs.[25]

Merton's second semester at Cambridge proved to be no better academically. In addition, his life became even more complicated when, as most biographers believe, he fathered a child. Although no record proves this conclusively, circumstantial evidence is overwhelming that it did in fact occur. That evidence is as follows. At the end of his first year of college, Merton traveled to New York to visit his grandparents. In June he received a letter from his godfather, Tom Bennett,[26] saying that Cambridge was threatening to revoke his scholarship and that it was best if Merton decided to stay in the United States. The letter came to Merton most likely because of his abysmal academic performance and the paternity issue.

Although it is unclear if a paternity suit was actually brought against Merton, it appears that Bennett did in fact arrange some kind of financial settlement with the pregnant woman, using a portion of Merton's trust.[27] In addition, Bennett agreed not to tell Thomas's family about this matter. This accounting of events is strongly supported by the fact that Merton told many of his friends that he had fathered a child, and that as a result he had to leave Cambridge. In fact, he told lifelong friend and later Columbia classmate Ed Rice that he had fathered a son but that both mother and child had been killed during the London Blitz.[28] While Merton may have believed that then, he evidently was not completely sure that had been their fate when he joined the Trappist order in 1944. As a part of making his simple profession, Merton had to write a will that would dispose of any remaining possessions. He still had a portion of his trust, and in the will requested that his sister-in-law receive half of his assets. The other half he bestowed to his godfather, Tom Bennett, with the instructions that this portion should be "paid by him to the person mentioned to him in my letters,

---

25. Ibid., 83.

26. Even though Merton would return to England briefly, he remained estranged from Bennett, and the two would never see each other again. Merton considered it to be one of the greatest regrets of his life (ibid., 87–89).

27. Ibid., 84–85.

28. Rice, *Man in the Sycamore Tree*, 9.

if that person can be contacted."[29] So, at least in 1944 Merton believed that it was possible that the mother and child may have still been alive.

While the evidence convincingly points to the fact that Merton did indeed father a child, it is a mystery as to who they were or what happened to them. It is perplexing that despite his prodigious journal keeping and frequent ruminating about his early past, there is not any kind of mention, even an oblique one, about his child. In addition, given Merton's enduring international fame, it is puzzling that no one ever came forward to claim they were the child or mother. In the end, it appears the specifics of this affair will remain a mystery. It seems clear, however, that this episode was a significant factor in encouraging Thomas to stay in America and make a fresh start.

In January 1935 Merton started Columbia University, and this time he had a successful college experience almost from the beginning.[30] He became involved with campus life and joined the Alpha Delta Phi fraternity. He was also not bashful about regaling his new friends with details of his wild time at Cambridge, bragging that his first sexual experience was with a Viennese prostitute he met at Hyde Park.[31] In addition, Merton also told many classmates that he had been virtually run out of England for fathering at least one illegitimate child.[32]

Merton also became politically active that year, joining the Young Communist League for a few months. However, by all accounts he was not very actively involved.[33] In addition, Thomas continued to become more involved with school activities, and in 1935 he began writing regularly for *Jester*, Columbia University's humor magazine. In fact, by the end of the next year he became its art editor. Merton served on the yearbook staff and also pursued athletics as a member of the cross-country team. Merton seemed to appreciate the second chance he had been given at Columbia and pursued all it had to offer with gusto.[34]

29. Mott, *Seven Mountains*, 90.

30. Ibid., 95.

31. Rice, *Man in the Sycamore Tree*, 36.

32. Mott, *Seven Mountains*, 95–96.

33. Ibid., 99–101.

34. Ibid., 101–2.

Premonastic Period

Merton suffered more loss in his life when his grandfather, Pop, died in October 1936. This was followed, ten months later, by the death of his grandmother, Bonnemaman.[35] Despite these losses he continued to apply himself to his studies and graduated from Columbia University in 1938. Thomas immediately began work on a master's degree, and would go on to write his master's thesis on William Blake.[36]

During this time Merton had a chance meeting with a Hindu monk in the summer of 1938 that actually led him to further explore Christianity. At the time this scholar and monk, Mahanambrata Brahmachari, was living in New York with some of Merton's friends.[37] During one of their many conversations Merton asked him what he should read to gain a better understanding of the spiritual and mystical life. Rather than recommending a Hindu text, Brahmachari suggested that Merton read Augustine's *Confessions* and Thomas à Kempis's *The Imitation of Christ*.[38]

In the fall of 1938, after a great deal of study and prayer, Merton decided to convert to Catholicism. While he had been baptized as a child, his upbringing was not especially religious. However, Merton had taken a class on Thomas Aquinas at Columbia, and that material, along with the books that Brahmachari had recommended, helped him reach his decision to become Catholic. Shortly after his conversion, in February 1939, he obtained his master's degree and decided to work on his doctorate at Columbia.[39]

The year 1939 marked the start of an interesting period of Merton's life. He was twenty-four and was traveling on what seemed like parallel

35. Ibid., 104.

36. Ibid., 112–15.

37. Brahmachari's story of how he came to the be in New York is a fascinating one. He had been sent to the United States to attend the World Congress of Religions that was being held in Chicago. Unfortunately, he arrived after the Congress had ended, and had no money to return home. He supported himself financially by speaking at various universities and churches. Brahmachari had made the acquaintance of one of Merton's friends, and in the summer of 1938 came to New York to stay with them (Merton, *Seven Storey Mountain* 209–13). Brahmachari already had a master's degrees in Sanskrit and Western philosophy from the University of Calcutta when he came to the United States. While here he went on to get his PhD from the University of Chicago. Brahmachari was from the Hindu tradition of neo-Vaisnavism, which affirmed devotion to the deity Vishnu and his many avatars (Niebuhr "Mahanambrata Brahmachari Is Dead at 95").

38. Merton, *Seven Storey Mountain*, 216.

39. Mott, *Seven Mountains*, 120–21.

trajectories. However, as will be seen, these seemingly disparate paths would later become one. On the one hand Merton was struggling mightily to be a successful writer. He had already written a handful of novels,[40] none of which was accepted for publication.[41] Merton had also been writing poetry for years and continued to do so during this period. In addition, in 1939 he supplemented his income by writing book reviews for the *New York Herald Tribune* and the *New York Times*.[42] In the spring of 1940 Merton secured Naomi Burton as his literary agent. She would remain his agent for the rest of Merton's life, and become a trusted friend and confidant.[43]

At this same time, Merton was trying to determine if he had a religious vocation. Ever since his conversion to Catholicism he had wondered if he was called to the priesthood. Merton had become friendly with his Thomistic philosophy professor, Dan Walsh, and he discussed the possibility of a clerical life with him. Walsh was very encouraging and in fact told him that he had always believed Merton had a religious vocation.[44] Walsh arranged for Merton to meet with local Franciscans, and Thomas submitted an application to enter the Franciscan order in the fall of 1939. Later, in the spring of 1940, Merton traveled to Havana, Cuba—part religious pilgrimage and part indulgence of his wanderlust. While attending mass there, he had what he believed was a profound religious experience. Merton described it in his journal, writing, "and so the unshakable certainty, the clear intermediate knowledge that Heaven was right in front of me, struck me like a thunderbolt and went through me like a flash of lightning and seemed to lift me clean up off the earth."[45]

Shortly after returning to America, Merton went to meet again with the Franciscans. This time he felt compelled to tell them the details about his wild past. While there is no clear record as to what he revealed, it is widely believed that it included the fact that he had fathered a child and engaged in a legal settlement.[46] During the conversation Merton was told

---

40. Some of these novels were titled *The Straits of Dover*, *The Labyrinth* (Merton, *Seven Storey Mountain* 263), and *The Man in the Sycamore Tree* (Mott, *Seven Mountains*, 126).

41. Merton submitted novels to Macmillan, Viking, Knopf, and Harcourt Brace; and all rejected his work (ibid., 147).

42. Merton, *Seven Storey Mountain*, 257.

43. Mott, *Seven Mountains*, 148.

44. Ibid., 122.

45. Merton, *Secular Journal*, 76–77.

46. Horan, *Franciscan Heart*, 70–72.

that it would be best if he withdrew his application to enter the Franciscan order.[47] Crestfallen, Merton decided to keep working on his PhD, and secured a job as an English instructor at Saint Bonaventure College in New York. Merton still felt called to the religious life, even if it would not be as a Franciscan priest, and made plans to become a member of the Third Order of Franciscans, a lay order.[48] In addition, he also bought a breviary, and in his own way attempted to live as a monk in the secular world, following the regimented prayer schedule found in a monastic community.[49]

During Christmas break 1940 Merton met again with his friend and former professor Dan Walsh. Walsh told Merton about a retreat he had recently made at a Trappist[50] monastery in Kentucky and encouraged Thomas to visit himself.[51] After some deliberation Merton made plans to make a retreat during Holy Week of the upcoming year at Our Lady of Gethsemani Trappist Monastery near Bardstown, Kentucky. He followed through with those plans and made this retreat from April 7 through April 14. He was greatly impressed with the glimpse of daily life there. As he described it in his autobiography,

> I was amazed at the way these monks, who were evidently just plain young Americans from the factories and colleges and farms and high-schools of the various states, were nevertheless absorbed and transformed in the liturgy. The thing that was most impressive was their absolute simplicity. They were concerned with one thing only: doing the things they had to do, singing what they had to sing, bowing and kneeling and so on when it was prescribed, and doing it as well as they could, without fuss or flourish or display. It was all utterly simple and unvarnished and straightforward, and I don't think I had ever seen anything, anywhere, so unaffected, so unself-conscious as these monks.[52]

Merton returned to New York and continued a process of discernment to discover if he truly had a religious vocation through the summer

47. Merton, *Seven Storey Mountain*, 325.

48. Mott, *Seven Mountains*, 328.

49. Merton, *Seven Storey Mountain*, 255.

50. The Trappist order is also known as the Order of the Cistercians of the Strict Observance. "Since this order was influenced by the Cistercians of a monastery in France called La Trappe, the monks of this order are known as Trappists" (Samway, ed., *Letters of Robert Giroux and Thomas Merton*, 24).

51. Ibid., 287–88.

52. Merton, *Seven Storey Mountain*, 361.

and fall of 1941. It is important to note that during this time Merton was also still actively trying to publish novels. While he was still unclear as to what he should do with his life, in November of that year he became even more uncertain when he was offered a position at Friendship House. Merton had been volunteering at Friendship House, an organization in Harlem dedicated to helping the poor, and was offered a full-time position there.[53] He was clearly at a crossroads as to what to do: work at the Friendship House, continue teaching and work to become a published writer, or try to live as a monk at Gethsemani? World events soon threatened to make his decision for him.

In 1941 the real possibility of being drafted into the military was on the mind of most young men, and Merton was no exception.[54] On December 1, he received a notice from the draft board informing him he had to appear for a second medical examination. Merton had already undergone one previous exam but was found to be ineligible for service at that time because of his extensive dental problems. However, as the war in Europe and the Pacific continued to rage, it seemed inevitable that he and his friends would soon be conscripted. With the call for this second medical exam, Merton believed it was likely he would now be deemed fit for service.[55] After more prayer and deliberation, Merton put his affairs in order, obtained a one-month extension for his draft board medical exam, gave away most of his belongings, and left New York. On December 10, 1941 he arrived at Our Lady of Gethsemani.[56]

Early Monastic Life and Loss of His Brother

Merton was accepted into the community as a novice monk, and his lascivious past was not deemed to be a bar into the monastic life there. The living conditions at the monastery in 1941 were intentionally primitive, with a strict meatless diet. His day consisted of study, prayer, and performing the manual labor that was needed to meet the physical needs of the community—chopping wood, working in the garden, and the like. Merton and his fellow monks had very little privacy. They all slept in a dormitory, with each having a small partitioned area in which to sleep. Merton's bed resembled a

53. Ibid., 358–59.
54. Merton, *Run to the Mountain*, 316–17.
55. Merton, *Seven Storey Mountain*, 340–43.
56. Mott, *Seven Mountains*, 201.

wooden bench and his mattress was a straw-filled pallet. Each of the monks took a vow of silence, and it was strictly enforced. Interestingly, the monks had developed their own kind of sign language that included over four hundred signs.[57]

In July 1942 Merton's brother, John Paul, came to visit the monastery. He had joined the Canadian Air Force and was serving as part of a bomber crew. John Paul asked to receive instruction to become a Catholic, and with the abbot's approval, began a week of intensive instruction about the faith, culminating with his baptism. This week would prove to be a special time for Thomas as it would be the last time he would see his brother. John Paul returned to his unit that was stationed in England and was killed on April 16, 1943, when his bomber was shot down over the English Channel.[58] The next day Merton was called to the abbot's office and given a telegram informing him that his brother was reported missing.[59]

The loss of his brother had a profound impact on Merton. He was twenty-seven, and all of his immediate family was dead. In addition, John Paul's death churned up a lifetime of memories and regrets. In his autobiography, Merton reflects upon the guilt and remorse he now felt for mistreating his younger brother when they were children. As Merton describes them, these memories of his brother were filled "with poignant compunction at the thought of my own pride and hard-heartedness, and his natural humility and love."[60] In recalling one childhood episode, Merton writes that he and his friends would sometimes build makeshift huts in the woods. John Paul, wanting to be with his older brother, would try to tag along. Merton describes how cruelly he treated his brother, and I quote at length from Merton's autobiography, as this marks a profound episode of suffering in Merton's life:

---

57. Ibid., 209–15.

58. Merton described the details of his brother's death:

"John Paul was severely injured in the crash, but he managed to keep himself afloat, and even tried to support the pilot, who was already dead. His companions had managed to float their rubber dinghy and pulled him in. He was very badly hurt: maybe his neck was broken. He lay in the bottom of the dinghy in delirium. He was terribly thirsty. He kept asking for water. But they didn't have any. The water tank had broken in the crash, and the water was all gone. It did not last too long. He had three hours of it, and then he died" (*Seven Storey Mountain*, 443).

59. Mott, *Seven Mountains*, 221–22.

60. Merton, *Seven Storey Mountain*, 24.

When I think now of that part of my childhood, the picture I get of my brother John Paul is this: standing in a field, about a hundred yards away from the clump of sumachs where we have built our hut, is this little perplexed five-year-old kid in short pants and a kind of a leather jacket, standing quite still, with his arms hanging down at his sides, and gazing in our direction, afraid to come any nearer on account of the stones, as insulted as he is saddened, and his eyes full of indignation and sorrow. And yet he does not go away. We shout at him to get out of there, to beat it, and go home, and wing a couple of more rocks in that direction, and he does not go away. We tell him to play in some other place. He does not move. And there he stands, not sobbing, not crying, but angry and unhappy and offended and tremendously sad. And yet he is fascinated by what we are doing, nailing shingles all over our new hut. And his tremendous desire to be with us and to do what we are doing will not permit him to go away. The law written in his nature says that he must be with his elder brother, and do what he is doing: and he cannot understand why this law of love is being so wildly and unjustly violated in his case.[61]

Monk, Writer, and a Search for Peace

When Merton entered the Trappist order, he was unsure about how he could be a writer and monk. He had written a number of poems prior to entering Gethsemani, and these remained in circulation with both his literary agent and friends, who continued searching for a publisher. These efforts paid off when, in November 1944, the poetry collection *Thirty Poems* was published.[62] Soon after this Merton met with the abbot at that time, Dom Frederick Dunne,[63] and told him he was struggling with whether or not he should write as a monk. His abbot informed him that he should indeed use these talents and continue writing poems and quickly followed up on that advice by giving Merton a series of writing assignments, including hagiographies of members of the order[64] as well as a history of

---

61. Merton, *Seven Storey Mountain*, 25.

62. Mott, *Seven Mountains*, 224.

63. Dom Frederick Dunne was a book lover and son of a book binder and publisher. Coady, *Merton and Waugh*, 16.

64. Merton, *Exile Ends in Glory*; and Merton, *What Are These Wounds?*

the monastic order.[65] Encouraged by his abbot, and buoyed by having his work published, he began a very prodigious amount of writing. In fact by 1947 Merton noted that he was working on no less than twelve different works.[66] One of these projects became the book that would forever change his life—*The Seven Storey Mountain*. While Merton was still a young man to write an autobiography, his life story and conversion to Catholicism was a compelling one. After being heavily edited by the Trappist censors, it was finally published by Harcourt Brace in October 1948. While the publisher believed it was a good book with an original printing of five thousand copies, they were not expecting the reception it would in fact receive.[67] In its first three months it sold almost fifty thousand copies. Its popularity only increased, at one point selling over ten thousand copies a week. Eventually, six hundred thousand copies of the original clothbound edition had been sold.[68] The success of the book was not due to initial press attention or a marketing campaign. Rather, its popularity grew almost completely from word-of-mouth recommendations. As *Time* magazine observed in the spring of 1949, "From the sedate lending libraries of New England to the bustling women's clubs of the West Coast, people are reading and talking about Poet Merton's sensitive, unhappy groping through the litter of modern civilization to find peace at last. Word-of-mouth endorsements are largely responsible for the demand."[69] This unlikely best seller would remain popular, going on to sell millions of copies.[70]

During this time Merton also began to suffer from a host of issues related to his emotional health.[71] They would recur for the rest of his life.

---

65. Merton, *Waters of Siloe*.

66. Merton, *Sign of Jonas*, 45.

67. Mott, *Seven Mountains*, 243.

68. Ibid., 247.

69. *Time*, "Religion: The Mountain."

70. Ostling, "Religion: Merton's Mountainous Legacy."

71. There is no attempt here to decide if Merton dealt with depression or mental illness, as clinically defined, throughout his life. I do allow, however, for Merton to speak for himself in the many occasions that he chronicles his mental and emotional well-being. It is in that regard that I broadly refer to these issues, in a purposefully nonclinical way, as his "emotional health." For further biographical exploration of these issues, see Mott, *Seven Mountains*, 291–345; Cooper, *Thomas Merton's Art of Denial*, 59–69; Moses, *Divine Discontent*, 161–82; Higgins, *Thomas Merton*, 42–43; Horan, *Franciscan Heart*, 75; and Gardner, *Only Mind Worth Having*, 111–25. For a psychiatric assessment of Merton based on his writings and biographical information, see the articles by Kramp, "Merton's Melancholia: Mother, Monasticism, and the Religion of Honor," and "Merton's

Merton was ordained a priest on May 26, 1949, and in July of that year Merton passed out while saying Mass. While the heat undoubtedly played a part, biographer Michael Mott believes it was a sign of burnout.[72] He points to the realization Merton expressed in his journals that ordination to the priesthood would not in itself lead to closer union with God but rather was another stage on the long journey he had been traveling, and would continue to do so. In addition, Mott argues Merton must have been feeling the pressure of following the success of *The Seven Storey Mountain*.[73] Merton chronicles this tumultuous period himself, writing,

> When the summer of my ordination ended, I found myself face to face with a mystery that was beginning to manifest itself in the depths of my soul and to move me with terror. Do not ask me what it was. I might apologize for it and call it "suffering." The word is not adequate because it suggests physical pain. That is not at all what I mean. It is true that something had begun to affect my health; but whatever happened to my health was only, it seems to me, an effect of this unthinkable thing that had developed in the depths of my being. And again: I have no way of explaining what it was. It was a sort of slow, submarine earthquake which produced strange commotions on the visible, psychological surface of my life. I was summoned to battle with joy and with fear, knowing in every case that the sense of battle was misleading, that my apparent antagonist was only an illusion, and that the whole commotion was simply the effect of something that had already erupted, without my knowing it, in the hidden volcano.[74]

In the fall of 1952 Merton candidly described the latest manifestation of these problems, writing, "Since my retreat I have been having another one of those nervous breakdowns. The same old familiar business. I am getting used to it now—since the old days in 1936, when I thought I was going to crack up on the Long Island Railroad, and the more recent one since ordination. And now this."[75] While not every mention of these problems will be chronicled in this chapter, I do include select entries to illustrate his ongoing problems.

Melancholia: Margie, Monasticism, and the Religion of Hope."

72. Mott, *Seven Mountains*, 254–55.

73. Ibid., 254.

74. Merton, *Sign of Jonas*, 230.

75. Merton, *Search for Solitude*, 2.

Merton also began to deal with a bevy of physical health issues beginning around this time. His gradually deteriorating health would be an issue that he focused more and more upon as he got older. In October and November of 1950 Merton had to go to the hospital in Louisville for surgery on a bone in his nose and treatment for colitis.[76] In addition, during this time lesions were discovered on his lungs; they appeared to be scars from his childhood bout with tuberculosis.[77]

Merton also began to actively seek more solitude, and living in community afforded very little of it. Towards this end he began exploring the possibilities of leaving Gethsemeni for another Trappist charter house, or even joining the Carthusian or Camaldoli orders, which provided much more solitude for their monks.[78] This desire for change also fits into a broader theme that can be seen in Merton's life. He did not ever feel truly settled, often thinking that if he could only change his surroundings, then he could grow closer to God, would be a better writer, would be his more authentic self, and so forth. As Merton scholar Robert Daggy puts it, Merton "suffered as much as any human from the 'grass is greener' syndrome."[79] Merton himself acknowledged this trait, writing in his journal, "The truth is, something inexplicable draws me away from here, something indefinable makes me uneasy here (I do not say unhappy)—always the old story of 'something missing.' What? Is it something essential? Won't there always be 'something missing'? Yet always that urge to 'go forth,' to leave, to take off for a strange land and start another life. Perhaps this is inevitable, just a desire one is supposed to have without fulfilling it."[80] Merton's longtime abbot, Dom James Fox, almost always denied Merton's requests to move to a different monastic order or accept invitations to attend conferences. This proved to be a source of no small amount of grief and frustration in Merton's life for decades to come.

The relationship between abbot Dom James Fox and Thomas Merton is a fascinating and complex one, perhaps best characterized by their mutual ambivalence. Dom James was born Harry Vincent Fox on December 10, 1896, in suburban Boston. His family was devoutly Catholic, and all

76. St. Joseph's Infirmary, on Eastern Parkway, no longer exists.

77. Mott, *Seven Mountains*, 264.

78. Grayston, *Thomas Merton and the Noonday Demon* provides a wonderful account of Merton's efforts to join this Italian order.

79. Merton, *Dancing in the Water of Life*, xv.

80. Merton, *Search for Solitude*, 285.

of his siblings would go on to have some kind of affiliation with religious communities. Fox was bright and attended Harvard, where he finished his undergraduate degree in three years. He then attended the Harvard graduate school of business administration. Fox was elected abbot in August of 1948 and served in that role for almost twenty years.[81] Many Merton biographers[82] have written at length about the relationship between Merton and his abbot. Perhaps Merton himself most succinctly captured the essence of their relationship in his journal when he wrote, "We are a pair of damned cats."[83] Merton believed that the abbot went out of his way to prevent him from exploring the opportunity for more solitude outside Gethsemani, and for attending conferences. He often saw these actions as the petty exercise of authority. Dom James, on the other hand, believed he was acting responsibly in exercising his authority and was in large part saving Merton from himself, as well as taking care of the rest of the community. To show both men's points of view, I have selected representative writing samples from each.

Merton wrote extensively in his journals about his frustration with his abbot, but also made them known to Dom James himself. I quote at length from a letter he wrote to him in 1959, which demonstrates the degree of frustration and resentment he often felt towards his abbot:

> I fully recognize your right to refuse permission for a leave of absence. In this you were following your conscience and within your rights. But I wonder about the way in which you have done everything possible to prevent me obtaining permission from anyone and in any way whatsoever. I do not deny you this right, but in point of fact it seems to me to represent an arbitrary and tyrannical spirit. Are you not so intent on your own views, in this matter, that you are willing to stifle the Holy Ghost in a soul? Do you not have an inordinate tendency to interfere in the workings of conscience and to suppress by violence those desires and ideals which run counter to your policies? Do you not tend to assume that your own policies represent the last word in the spiritual perfection of every one of your subjects? . . . I have always striven to be perfectly obedient to legitimate commands in the external forum, but I beg the right to form my conscience according to the guidance of my

81. Lipsey, *Make Peace before the Sun Goes Down*, 9–15.

82. Lipsey's *Make Peace before the Sun Goes Down* focuses exclusively on this relationship and provides a fascinating, comprehensive and balanced accounting of it.

83. Merton, *Learning to Love*, 108.

directors, in the internal forum, without demands that I follow your directions and no other. I hope you understand this rightly as a humble and filial petition.[84]

Dom James saw things differently. In the following portion of a letter to the superior of the entire order, Dom Gabriel Sortais, Fox shows he believed he was acting to help Merton:

> Father Louis knows that his troubles do not come from his Trappist surroundings in general, and Gethsemani in particular. He knows, because he practically admitted it to me, that his problems are all inside himself. But as neurotics usually do, they blame everybody and everything else for their interior suffering. His problem is that he would like to be without any restraint or discipline over him, so that he could always do what he wished. But if he were in such a position, where would his spiritual life be? Where would his sanctification be? And he knows that very well.[85]

Fox also had the well-being of his community and fellow monks to consider, and he saw Merton's departure to another monastic community as being problematic. Merton was well thought of and admired by many, especially younger, monks. In describing the impact on them Fox wrote, "They look upon him as an oracle of spirituality and lean heavily upon him for their guidance in the spiritual life. If he ever were to leave here, it would be a source of great scandal to our young professed and would betray them into the spirit of instability and change. I can hardly picture what the results of his change from here would be."[86] It is important to point out that while the relationship was often contentious, there was also a bond of mutual respect and care. It is no small irony to a visitor at the Gethsemani cemetery today to see Dom James buried next to Merton's grave.

In 1953 in an effort to accommodate Merton's desire for more solitude, Dom James allowed him to use an abandoned toolshed on the monastery grounds, dubbed St. Anne's. He was only allowed to spend a few hours a day there, and it was not his to use exclusively.[87] Merton continued to long for greater solitude and to live more of an eremitical lifestyle. In 1955 Dom James offered to let him live in a nearby fire tower. This would provide Merton the solitude he had been asking for, while also offering a

---

84. Merton, *Witness to Freedom*, 216.

85. Lipsey, *Make Peace before the Sun Goes Down*, 65.

86. Grayston, *Thomas Merton and the Noonday Demon*, 123–24.

87. Mott, *Seven Mountains*, 274.

valuable service to the monastic community and surrounding county. The only stipulation was that Merton could do no writing of any kind, could not keep a notebook or have a typewriter, for the next five years. When faced with this reality, Merton quickly dropped those plans and in fact volunteered for a newly vacant position as master of novices, teaching the new monks.[88]

Merton enjoyed his work with the novices and by all accounts did a fine job with their instruction.[89] His instruction focused on their practical spiritual formation rather than solely academic matters.[90] During this time Merton also continued writing, his active prayer schedule, and other assigned tasks at the monastery. In addition, he was able to receive books from friends, and was a voracious reader, devouring several books at one time. His interests included world literature, Western and Eastern theology, and even nuclear physics.[91]

On March 15, 1958 Merton had what he considered to be a profound religious experience. While in Louisville meeting with a printer about a monastic publication, he came to a crowded downtown intersection, Fourth and Walnut. Merton, who had spent most of the last seventeen years separated from the rest of world, suddenly felt connected, in a real and intimate way, to the rest of humanity. As he described some time later,

> In Louisville, at the corner of Fourth and Walnut, in the center of the shopping district, I was suddenly overwhelmed with the realization that I loved all those people, that they were mine and I theirs, that we could not be alien to one another even though we were total strangers. It was like waking from a dream of separateness, of spurious self-isolation in a special world, the world of renunciation and supposed holiness. The whole illusion of a separate holy existence is a dream. Not that I question the reality of my vocation, or of my monastic life: but the conception of "separation from the world" that we have in the monastery too easily presents itself as a complete illusion: the illusion that by making vows we become a different species of being, pseudoangels, "spiritual men," men of interior life, what have you.[92]

88. Cooper, *Thomas Merton's Art of Denial*, 56–57.

89. Mott, *Seven Mountains*, 288–89.

90. Grayston, *Thomas Merton and the Noonday Demon*, 27.

91. Mott, *Seven Mountains*, 307.

92. Merton, *Conjectures of a Guilty Bystander*, 156–57.

While this experience would have a long-lasting effect on Merton's life, he was also once again "feeling all the old symptoms of stress: insomnia, colitis, headaches."[93] In addition, he was also exploring the possibility of moving to another monastic community, this time in Central America.

The year 1960 saw the birth of new friendships in Merton's life and an expansion of the issues he addressed in his writing. He began seeing a Louisville psychiatrist, Jim Wygal, for a regular series of psychoanalysis sessions. This relationship would change from interaction between doctor and patient into a friendship. These regular visits meant Merton would be making more regular trips to Louisville, which increasingly included excursions to Wygal's house to listen to jazz records, as well as to jazz clubs.[94] In addition, while continuing to write about contemplation and solitude, Merton began to focus on a variety of social ills humanity was facing. During this time Merton also continued his exploration of Zen and Buddhism, which will be explored at length in chapter 4.

Merton also continued to struggle with his emotional health as well. In his journals he candidly chronicles these problems. "And so my own neurosis runs like a sore, and I know it, and see it, and see that I am helpless to do anything about it! And am, of course, guilty. So it is that the Christian and monastic mind is admirably fitted to be a seed ground of neurosis. This is at once a weakness and a strength. Unfortunately I can't imagine, for the moment, where to find any kind of strength in this futility."[95] Continuing to struggle with the same issues, less than a week later he wrote, "Anyway, I am worn down. I am easily discouraged. The depressions are deeper, more frequent. I am near fifty. People think I am happy."[96]

The Hermitage Years and the Affair

A movement began at Gethsemani to host representatives from other Christian faiths in an effort to foster a growing spirt of ecumenism. In order to meet those needs, while avoiding unnecessary disruption to the community routine, plans were made to construct a small building to serve as a conference center on the monastery grounds. Before construction began, Merton's abbot agreed that this space would also be an ideal place for

93. Mott, *Seven Mountains*, 329.

94. Moses, *Divine Discontent*, 4.

95. Merton, *Turning toward the World*, 321.

96. Ibid., 323.

Merton to achieve the solitude he craved. Initially, Dom James would only allow him to visit it periodically. However, over time Merton was gradually allowed to spend more time at the concrete-block building that would, in time, become his permanent home: Our Lady of Mount Carmel Hermitage.

A few entries from Merton's journals during this time illustrate the ebullient sense of the excitement and peace he felt in this place. An entry from late September 1963 reflects this: "Yesterday went up to the hermitage and sat on the grass and in the tall trees. The house quiet and cool. A few birds. And nothing. Who would want to live in any other way?"[97] Merton was allowed to spend more time at the hermitage, and in October 1964 was allowed to spend the night there for the first time. As his journal indicates, the experience lived up to his expectations, "Got up there about nightfall. Wonderful silence, saying Compline gently and slowly with a candle burning before the icon of Our Lady. A deep sense of peace and truth. That this was the way things are supposed to be, that I was in my right mind for a change . . . Total absence of care and agitation. Slept wonderfully well . . . I felt very much alive, and real, and awake, surrounded by silence and penetrated by truth."[98] Finally, late in the summer of 1965, Dom James granted Merton permission to live full time at the hermitage. His official first day as a hermit was August 20, 1965.[99] After spending time there Merton wrote about how this place seemed to finally be the right fit for him:

> Everything about this hermitage simply fills me with joy . . . it is the place God has given me after so much prayer and longing— but without my deserving it—and it is a delight. I can imagine no other joy on earth than to have such a place and to be at peace in, to live in silence, to think and write, to listen to the wind and to all the voices of the wood, to live in the shadow of the big cedar cross, to prepare for my death and my exodus to the heavenly country, to love my brothers and all people, and to pray for the whole world and for peace and good sense among men. So it is "my place" in the scheme of things, and that is sufficient![100]

Merton had finally attained the relative solitude and isolation that he had craved.

---

97. Merton, *Dancing in the Water of Life*, 20.

98. Ibid., 154.

99. Ibid., xiv.

100. Ibid., 209.

During these years Merton also continued to battle a variety of medical issues. In the fall of 1964 what was originally thought to be an ordinary case of poison ivy turned out to be a skin disease that was related to anxiety.[101] That condition worsened to such a state that by February of 1965 Merton had to wear dermal gloves. He described this painful condition in his journal, "The skin of my hands erupted again, leafed and cracked, deep holes in the skin are quite painful. It interferes with work. Even tying shoes is painful. Wore gloves to make my bed. Mess!"[102] He was also dealing with stomach illnesses, often treating himself by drinking Twining's Lapsang Souchong tea that a friend from Louisville had brought him.[103] However, these stomach problems continued, and by June he was diagnosed with a staphylococcus infection in his intestines. Antibiotics, diagnostic testing, and a weeklong stay in a Louisville hospital did not fully relieve his problems. These continuing health problems, and the reality that he was no longer a healthy young man, are clearly expressed in a journal entry around this time. Merton had found an old photograph of himself playing rugby at Cambridge, and he writes:

> I can see that that was a different body from the one I have now—one entirely young and healthy, one that did not know sickness, weakness, anguish, tension, fatigue—a body totally assured of itself and without care . . . And now what kind of a body! An arthritic hip; a case of chronic dermatitis on my hands for a year and a half (so that I have to wear gloves); sinusitis, chronic ever since I came to Kentucky; lungs always showing up some funny shadow or other on ex-rays (though not lately); perpetual diarrhea and a bleeding anus; most of my teeth gone; most of my hair gone; a chewed-up vertebra in my neck which causes my hands to go numb and my shoulder to ache—and for which I sometimes need traction.[104]

Merton's health problems only worsened during this time, with his back becoming the top concern. Although he had struggled with back and neck problems for years, conservative care could no longer provide relief. Merton was admitted to St. Joseph's Infirmary in March 1966 for

---

101. Mott, *Seven Mountains*, 403.

102. Merton, *Dancing in the Water of Life*, 209.

103. Ibid., 229.

104. Ibid., 326.

back surgery.[105] While recovering there he met a student-nurse, M, from Cincinnati.[106] The two struck up a friendship during his stay there, and that relationship would continue after he returned to Gethsemani. In fact, it quickly became a romantic one, with elaborately arranged meetings in Louisville. The two also supplemented their time together with phone calls and voluminous letter writing, with each declaring their love for the other. While this affair only lasted several months, it had a profound impact on the last years of Merton's life.[107] He believed that he had finally found feminine love, something that he thought he had never experienced in his life.[108]

Merton's relationship with M helped reaffirm that his role in this world was that of a monk. No matter how dysfunctional at times he found his monastic order to be,[109] his place was in it, not out in the secular world. While there is no evidence that Merton ever seriously considered leaving the religious life, this was certainly the time to do it if he was ever so inclined. This internationally famous author had found the love of a beautiful and intelligent woman who was prepared to run away with him and get married; if he would only ask.[110] Instead, Merton chose the familiarity of his cloister and his calling to live as a priest and monk. Although Merton and M continued to exchange sporadic letters and phone calls into 1968, the relationship was for all practical purposes over in the fall of 1966.[111] This fascinating episode of Merton's life is covered extensively in chapter 4.

Merton resumed his usual activities of writing, responding to the mountains of correspondence he received on a daily basis,[112] and visiting

---

105. Neurosurgeon Thomas M. Marshall performed an anterior cervical fusion in order to correct Merton's cervical spondylosis (Higgins, *Thomas Merton*, 77).

106. Merton's account of this relationship in his journals is one sided, and editors have rightly decided to keep this woman's identity private, referring to her simply as M. While her name has been published in some biographies, I also choose the same moniker, M.

107. Merton himself uses the term "affair" to describe the relationship many times in his journal *Learning to Love*, 63, 70, 88, 90, 108, and 122.

108. Merton, *Dancing in Water of Life*, 259–60.

109. See Merton's call for monastic renewal in the article, "Monk in Diaspora" for his thoughts about the current state and future of Catholic monasticism.

110. Merton, *Learning to Love*, 54–55.

111. Mott, *Seven Mountains*, 468.

112. Merton was a prolific letter writer, exchanging over ten thousand letters with approximately 2,100 people. (Gardner, *Only Mind Worth Having*, 2–3) Merton wrote to religious figures (e.g., Karl Rahner, Rosemary Radford Reuther, Thich Nhat Hanh, D. T. Suzuki), those devoted to social justice and peace (e.g., Dorothy Day and Daniel

with guests to his hermitage. During this time Merton was increasingly focused on issues outside the monastery. He continued writing about the war in Vietnam, nuclear proliferation, and a host of social ills facing society in the mid 1960s. Merton also continued to have health problems, and after being treated conservatively for bursitis, entered a hospital in late February 1967 for elbow surgery. Unfortunately the surgery was not successful, leaving him in a great deal of pain.[113] Luckily technology had advanced to the point that he was able to get a tape recorder, which he used to dictate some of his correspondence and other writings, which were transcribed by fellow monks.

On September 7, 1967, Merton received news that would considerably change his life. The long-serving abbot, Dom James Fox, was resigning from that position, and Merton was overjoyed about the change in leadership. Interestingly, he was concerned enough at the prospect of being chosen to lead the community himself that he posted a tongue-in-cheek letter, "MY CAMPAIGN PLATFORM," writing that he was not fit for the job because he was not a good administrator, had no business acumen, and was not "equipped to spend the rest of my life arguing about complete trivialities with one hundred and twenty-five slightly confused and anxiety ridden monks."[114] His observations about his fellow monks offended several members of his community.

An abbotical election was held in January of 1968, and Fr. Flavian Burns was elected the new head of the monastic community. Merton was elated, as he had taught Burns when he was a novice monk. Merton's horizons soon opened wide when the new abbot granted him permission to travel to the types of conferences he had been denied in the past.

Merton accepted an invitation from the Aide á l'Implantation Monastique organization, a Benedictine group that worked for monastic renewal. They planned a conference in Bangkok in December 1968, and Merton was invited to be a speaker. While in Asia, Merton would have an opportunity to immerse himself in Buddhism and explore other monastic traditions, all with the hope that he would return home and share those learnings with his own community. In addition, Merton was also granted permission to

---

Berrigan), other writers (e.g., Boris Pasternak, John Howard Griffin), and celebrities (e.g., Joan Baez and members of the Kennedy family). Hundreds of these letters have been published in a variety of books, with many others collected at the Thomas Merton Center at Bellarmine University.

113. Merton, *Learning to Love*, 201–10.

114. Mott, *Seven Mountains*, 503–4.

visit various monastic communities in the United States.[115] In May he spent two weeks at monasteries on the California coast and New Mexico desert before his trip abroad.

That old and persistent feeling of restlessness also returned. Around this time Merton was finding that life at his hermitage was not as fulfilling as it once had been. The solitude he had longed for was increasingly disturbed by a parade of visitors—many invited, some others not. Word had spread that Merton was living apart from the community, and many people discovered ways to avoid the monastery gates to reach his hermitage. These interlopers included spiritual seekers, students and clergy interested in Merton's work, and occasionally the mentally deranged. He humorously described one of these encounters in his journal: "The other night when it was too hot to go to bed, I was sitting up with nothing on but a pair of underpants when a couple of admirers suddenly appeared in front of the cottage. I told them to get the hell out, thereby once again ruining my image."[116]

Coda

In July of 1968 more of his time was occupied with preparation for his trip to Asia. There were many details to sort out, including trips to Louisville for required inoculations.[117] On September 10 he left Gethsemani to begin his journey. His itinerary was somewhat open-ended; his abbot agreed to consider changes to his schedule based on other offers to travel that might be made while Merton was on the trip.[118] What no one could have known was that this was the last day Thomas Merton would spend at Gethsemani.

Merton first spent time at monastic communities in New Mexico, Alaska, and California. He gave conferences to the other monks and religious and also explored surrounding areas for possible future hermitages.[119] Finally, on October 15 he set off for Asia. In his journal Merton describes his elation at finally embarking on a trip that he had dreamed of for years:

---

115. Horan, *Franciscan Heart*, 50.
116. Merton, *Other Side of the Mountain*, 129.
117. Ibid., 143–46.
118. Mott, *Seven Mountains*, 537.
119. Ibid., 541.

The moment of take-off was ecstatic. The dewy wing was suddenly covered with rivers of cold sweat running backward. The window wept jagged shining courses of tears. Joy. We left the ground—I with Christian mantras and a great sense of destiny, of being at last on my true way after years of waiting and wondering and fooling around . . . I am going home, to the home where I have never been in this body.[120]

Merton arrived in Bangkok, and after a couple days of rest he left for Calcutta. Once there he was overwhelmed with the crush of people and grinding poverty.[121] A trip to New Delhi and other parts of India soon followed. On November 1st, he took a train from New Delhi to Dharamsala, where the Dalai Lama resided. Months before, arrangements had been made for the two to meet. Over the course of a week they met on three separate occasions. Merton recorded in his journals that the Dalai Lama told him he was familiar with his writings. After discussing Merton's interest in Tibetan mysticism, the Dalai Lama recommended that Merton meet with a qualified Tibetan scholar who could unite study and practice.[122]

Two days later Merton and the Dalai Lama met again. Merton notes that most of their discussions during this visit centered on Eastern and Western comprehension of knowledge and understanding. However, their meeting included more than a discussion about epistemology. Interestingly, also during this encounter the Dalai Lama demonstrated the Tibetan meditation posture. Merton describes that this second meeting went very well, and that both men had enjoyed themselves, with a promise to meet again in two days.[123] On November 5th, the two met again for the last time. They continued their conversation about the various approaches to knowledge, and compared details of the daily lives of Western and Buddhist monks. Merton believed this was the best of their three visits and wrote in his journal that "it was a very warm and cordial discussion and at the end I felt we had become very good friends and were somehow quite close to one another. I feel great respect and fondness for him as a person and I believe, too, that there is a real spiritual bond between us."[124]

---

120. Merton, *Other Side of the Mountain*, 205.

121. Ibid., 216.

122. Merton, *Asian Journal*, 112–13.

123. Ibid., 113.

124. Ibid., 125.

On November 29th, Merton arrived in Colombo, Ceylon (now Sri Lanka). A few days later he would have a religious experience that is reminiscent of the one that he had at Fourth and Walnut in Louisville, as well as the one in Cuba some twenty-eight years before. It is similar in terms of how it seemed to open his eyes to a new understanding about the nature of being and his place in the world. This occurred on December 4 when Merton had an opportunity to visit Polonnaruwa to see the famous statues of the Buddhas. Merton described this experience a few days later in his traveling journal. While it is a long entry, it is important to let Merton describe the event, to speak for himself:

> Looking at these figures I was suddenly, almost forcibly, jerked clean out of the habitual, half-tied vision of things, and an inner clearness, clarity, as if exploding from the rocks themselves, became evident and obvious. The queer evidence of the reclining figure, the smile, the sad smile of Ananda standing with arms folded (much more "imperative" than Da Vinci's Mona Lisa because completely simple and straightforward). The thing about all this is that there is no puzzle, no problem, and really no "mystery." All problems are resolved and everything is clear, simply because what matters is clear. The rock, all matter, all life, is charged with dharmakaya—everything is emptiness and everything is compassion. I don't know when in my life I have ever had such a sense of beauty and spiritual validity running together in one aesthetic illumination. Surely, with Mahabalipuram and Polonnaruwa my Asian pilgrimage has come clear and purified itself. I mean, I know and have seen what I was obscurely looking for. I don't know what else remains but I have now seen and have pierced through the surface and have got beyond the shadow and the disguise. This is Asia in its purity, not covered over with garbage, Asian or European or American, and it is clear, pure, complete. It says everything; it needs nothing. And because it needs nothing it can afford to be silent, unnoticed, undiscovered.[125]

It would have been interesting to see how Merton would have processed and reflected further on this experience as he continued his trip and eventually returned to Gethsemani. Unfortunately, that was not meant to be as he would be dead within the week.

Merton finally returned to Bangkok for his conference, after a brief stop in Singapore, on December 7th. The conference started two days later,

125. Ibid., 233–36.

and on December 10, 1968, Merton gave a presentation titled "Marxism and Monastic Perspectives."[126] He ended his remarks by saying, "So I will disappear from view and we can all have a Coke or something. Thank you very much."[127] Those were his last words recorded or written. After lunch Merton returned to the cottage that he and a few other monks were sharing at the conference center. Around 4:00 p.m. another priest, Father Francois de Grunne, who was also staying at that cottage, went to Merton's room to fetch a key for another room. After knocking repeatedly with no answer, Fr. de Grunne looked through the louvres in the top part of the door and saw Merton laying on the floor. De Grunne and three others struggled to break into the room, and once successful, found Merton laying on his back, in his underwear, with a five foot tall fan laying diagonally across his body. There was a long raw burn mark across his body. He was unresponsive, and his face was discolored and feet curled up. A doctor soon arrived and pronounced him dead. An investigation was quickly done and found that the fan in question had a faulty cord. It is believed that Merton had returned to his room and took a shower before taking a nap. After he got out of the shower he touched the fan while standing on a wet tile floor and was electrocuted. Thomas Merton was dead at the age of fifty-three.[128] It is interesting to note that he had entered Gethsemani on that date, exactly twenty-seven years earlier.

Conclusion

Thomas Merton is a remarkably complex figure. His life story and diverse interests continue to make him a fascinating character for a wide variety of people. At first blush, it may appear that Merton lived a life foreign to most of us, existing on the margins of society in the woods of Kentucky. However, because he produced scores of books and journals, readers are able to discover a figure that is eminently relatable. In exploring his writings, one finds that Merton in fact lived in a way similar to most of us. It was a life of triumph and defeat, joy and frustration, contentment and longing, love and loss; it was a full life.

A survey of Merton's life shows that he was no stranger to suffering. He lost his mother at the age of six, and lived an itinerant and often chaotic

126. Mott, *Seven Mountains*, 563.

127. Ibid., 564.

128. Mott, *Seven Mountains*, 564–67.

life with his father, until he too passed away when Thomas was fifteen. As a young adult Merton nearly squandered his opportunity for a quality college education because of his riotous behavior. His adult life was often marked by a constant striving for a state of being that always seemed just out of reach, a longing for something he would never attain. In addition, Merton often chafed at the restrictions imposed on him by his superiors. Finally, he suffered from a host of issues that impacted his physical and emotional well-being.

One needs to be careful not to overemphasize the suffering in Merton's life. That has not been my aim here, as he certainly experienced a great many instances of contentment, joy, and peace. However, given the scope of this book, Merton's understanding of why an all-loving and all-powerful God allows suffering in this world, to examine the theme of suffering in his own life is important. It is within that context that one can then better explore his thoughts about God's role in human suffering, or theodicy. The following chapter provides some additional foundational work, briefly examining modern theodicies so that Merton's own thoughts on the subject can then be better understood and contextualized.

2

Theodicy Survey

The problem of evil, or theodicy question, is one that thinkers throughout history have struggled to address. Specifically, how does one reconcile belief in a God who is all-powerful, all-knowing, and all-good in light of all the gratuitous evil and suffering seen throughout history? Philosophers, theologians, and artists have attempted to solve that riddle, and this questioning continues today. In this chapter I examine four prominent Christian responses to the problem of evil: free will, soul making, process, and cruciform theodicies. In addition, since Thomas Merton was increasingly immersed in Zen thought towards the end of his life, I also review some of the responses to suffering found in the Zen tradition. It is important to point out that this short yet dense chapter does not present all the subtle nuances of each theory, or their critiques—of which there are many.[1] Rather, the intent is to provide a concise summary of each theodicy. This examination of the problem of evil, and prominent responses to it, is an important task so that the later exploration of Thomas Merton's conception of evil and suffering, and how it fits into God's divine plan, can be properly contextualized and understood.

1. See Davis, ed., *Encountering Evil*, for a full and balanced summary and critique of these Christian theodicies.

Theodicy Defined

The term *theodicy* is derived from the Greek words for "God" (*theos*) and "justice" (*dikē*) and was first introduced by philosopher Gottfried Wilhelm Leibniz (1641–1716).[2] Whereas Leibniz may have coined the term, the question of why God allows evil and suffering has been with humanity since the dawn of civilization. The book of Job, for example, deals extensively with this topic as the embattled Job seeks to find meaning in his suffering. The appeal of that piece of Scripture stems from the universal nature of the questions posed by the tormented Job. In addition, various secular writers have also dealt with the issue of God's role in evil and suffering throughout the centuries.

Finally, it is important to properly identify the role of theodicy. It cannot, nor should it, be thought of as delivering a final, definitive answer to the problem of evil. Rather, theodicy provides resources to better engage the problem. In particular, Christian theodicies do not seek to offer conclusive solutions but instead cull through Scripture and theological tradition to address the issue. As theologian Mark S. M. Scott writes about Christian approaches to the problem of evil:

> Theodicy honestly acknowledges the mystery of evil, but that acknowledgment does not mark the end of the conversation. If that were so, other Christian doctrines shrouded in mystery—the Trinity, the human and divine nature of Christ, the relationship between providence and free will—would foreclose conversation rather than stimulate it, and the history of theology has shown us otherwise on these controversies. There is too much at stake to walk away from the conversation, and theology has resources to speak to the problem even if it cannot "solve" it. The language of "solution" befits mathematics and the other hard sciences, not Christian theology.[3]

Free Will Theodicy

Free will theodicy is rooted in the theology of Saint Augustine (354–430 CE). For centuries it was the dominant theory and "was the central prism

2. O'Collins and Farrugia, "Theodicy," 262.
3. Scott, *Pathways in Theodicy*, 4.

through which theologians reflected on the problem of evil."[4] Augustine argued that moral evil entered the world because of the human abuse of free will, as described in the Genesis account of Adam and Eve.[5] In addition, in the late twentieth century, philosopher Alvin Plantinga developed an argument that the presence of evil and suffering in the world was not logically incompatible with a God who is both all-loving and all-powerful. Plantinga was responding to arguments that posited that the problem of evil was prima facie evidence that the traditional understanding of an all-loving, all-powerful God was logically impossible. In particular, he was seeking to rebut the arguments made by philosopher J. L. Mackie.

In his seminal 1955 article, "Evil and Omnipotence," Mackie argues that "in its simplest form the problem is this: God is omnipotent; God is wholly good; and yet evil exists. There seems to be some contradiction between these three propositions, so that if any two of them were true the third would be false."[6] He affirms that an all-loving God who could eliminate evil would in fact do so. Mackie critiques tenets of several classic theistic responses to the problem of evil, arguing that in their attempts to provide a satisfactory response, they are forced to redefine the meaning of God's omnipotence or benevolence, or the nature and reality of evil. After this examination Mackie concludes that "This study strongly suggests that there is no valid solution to the problem which does not modify at least one of the constituent propositions in a way which would seriously affect the essential core of the theistic position."[7]

Plantinga responds directly to Mackie in his classic 1974 work, *God, Freedom, and Evil*. He did not intend to do the work of a theodicy proper. Rather, Plantinga states that a theodicist endeavors to show God's reason for permitting evil, while his task is more modest. Plantinga only wishes to logically demonstrate that Mackie's three premises—that God is omnipotent, that God is wholly good, and that evil exists—are not contradictory. Whether the idea is true that God is wholly good "is quite beside the point."[8]

Toward that end of his book, Plantinga formulates an approach that he names the free will defense. As will be seen, its name derives from the

4. Ibid., 95.

5. Augustine's notion of original sin and fallenness is discussed at length in the next chapter.

6. Mackie, "Evil and Omnipotence," 200.

7. Ibid., 212.

8. Plantinga, *God, Freedom, and Evil*, 28.

importance that human freedom plays. Plantinga works to demonstrate that the existence of evil in the world does not necessarily invalidate a belief in an all-powerful and all-loving God. He begins by criticizing Mackie, arguing that he failed to make his logical case in any detail.[9] To counter that, Plantinga uses many logical arguments to demonstrate that the existence of evil does not necessarily preclude the possibility of a God who is both all-loving and all-powerful. He affirms that a belief in God's omnipotence is to be understood as God having the power to do all that is logically possible. God, he argues, cannot do the impossible—cannot make a square circle or a married bachelor. Plantinga goes on to argue that God cannot create a world containing moral good without creating one that also contains moral evil.[10] For creating truly free creatures brings with it the risk of the abuse of free will, thus leading to evil and suffering. As Plantinga writes, "God could have created a world containing no moral evil only by creating one without significantly free persons."[11] Plantinga concisely encapsulates his argument as follows:

> A world containing creatures who are significantly free (and freely perform more good than evil actions) is more valuable, all else being equal, than a world containing no free creatures at all. Now God can create free creatures, but He can't cause or determine them to do only what is right. For if He does so, then they aren't significantly free after all; they do not do what is right freely. To create creatures capable of moral good, therefore, He must create creatures capable of moral evil; and He can't give these creatures the freedom to perform evil and at the same time prevent them from doing so. As it turned out, sadly enough, some of the free creatures God created went wrong in the exercise of their freedom; this is the source of moral evil. The fact that free creatures sometimes go wrong, however, counts neither against God's omnipotence nor against His goodness; for He could have forestalled the occurrence of moral evil only by removing the possibility of moral good.[12]

In his essay "Free Will and Evil," Stephen T. Davis, an evangelical Christian, builds upon Plantinga's work to present his version of the

9. Ibid., 23.

10. Ibid., 44.

11. Ibid., 53.

12. Plantinga, *God, Freedom, and Evil*, 30.

Augustinian free will theodicy.[13] According to Davis, God is affirmed to be omnipotent and perfectly good while at the same time acknowledging that evil is indeed a metaphysical reality. Davis's free will argument posits that God had two principal goals in creating the universe. First, God wanted to create the best world possible in which there is a greater amount of good than evil. Second, God sought to create a world where morally free human beings would freely and lovingly decide to obey God. Therefore, God created a world that was originally free of evil, but also created sentient beings capable of exercising free moral choice.[14]

Theodicies typically address two different kinds of evil: moral and natural. Moral evil can be conceived of as the suffering that results from the free actions of human beings. Theologically, this type of evil has been associated with suffering that results from sinful states or activities, including pride, envy, lying, murder, greed, and the like. Natural evil, on the other hand, encompasses the pain and suffering that result from natural events such as floods, earthquakes, diseases, famines and other natural disasters.[15]

In addressing moral evil, Davis affirms that in making humans who possess free will, God ran the risk that individuals could choose to do evil. Thus, the possibility of freely doing evil is the unavoidable consequence of creating beings that were also truly free to do good. As Davis argues, humans did indeed choose to sin. Seen in this way, the free will theodicy asserts that God is not responsible for moral evil. Rather, this Augustinian notion of fallenness, or the human abuse of free will, is the cause. God, therefore, is not directly responsible for moral evil.[16] As Davis states, "All the moral evil that exists in the world is due to the choices of free moral agents whom God created, and no other world which God could have created would have had a better balance of good over evil than the actual world will have."[17]

Theodicy typically also address the problem of natural evil and suffering. Here, free will theodicy must expand its argument since the human abuse of free will rarely causes or contributes to the suffering caused by natural disasters and illness. A traditional theistic understanding of God affirms that he has indeed become directly involved at times in human

13. Davis, "Free Will and Evil," 74.

14. Ibid., 73.

15. Davis, "Introduction," xi.

16. Davis, "Free Will and Evil," 75.

17. Ibid., 76.

history. However, the free will theodicy argues that in order for the universe to be one of regular and dependable laws, such divine intervention must by necessity be infrequent. Therefore, in the face of natural disasters, God must let nature take its course in most circumstances. In addition, Davis's free will theodicy posits that it is for the best that God created a world in which some pain results from nonhuman causes. While at first this may seem insensitive or even cruel, Davis argues that that is not the case. He believes there would be almost no sense of morality or ability to differentiate good from evil in a world in which there is no pain and the only human experience in life is that of pleasure. As he puts it, "pain shows us that something is wrong with our lives, that something more is needed."[18] In addition, Davis believes some spiritual good and growth often comes from suffering.[19]

In examining his own theory, Davis asks if one could not look at history, with its innumerable examples of evil and suffering, and conclude that God's divine plan has gone horribly wrong. He affirms that it in fact has not. Davis believes that God's decision to create morally imperfect beings, capable of sinning, will turn out to be a wise one, "because the good that will in the end result from it will outweigh the evil that will in the end result from it. In the eschaton it will be evident that God chose the best course and that the favorable balance of good over evil that will then exist was obtainable by God in no other way or in no morally preferable way."[20] Davis emphasizes that ultimately, God will redeem all suffering and evil. He states that God uses evil causally in some cases to help produce a greater good, e.g., the pain an athlete feels while strengthening her body, pain from a surgery that restores a person to health, and so forth.[21] Davis believes that this kind of suffering is easily justified.

What about evil and suffering that appear to be gratuitous? He defines this kind of evil as "evil that the world, in the long run and all things considered, would be better without."[22] Davis argues that gratuitous evil and suffering may initially appear to be unjustified. However, he affirms that with the perspective of time, all evils initially believed to be gratuitous can be seen as events that actually lead to some greater good. Finally, for

18. Davis, "Free Will and Evil," 79.

19. Ibid., 78–79.

20. Ibid., 75.

21. Ibid., 83–84.

22. Ibid., 84.

those instances of truly gratuitous suffering, most notably the Holocaust, one must look to the eschaton and the ushering in of the kingdom of God, when those types of evils will "pale into insignificance next to 'the glory that is to be revealed to us.'"[23]

Soul-Making Theodicy

The second theodicy to be examined is the so-called soul-making model. This theory was developed and popularized by theologian John Hick in his classic 1966 book, *Evil and the God of Love*. Hick's theodicy relies heavily on the thought of Saint Irenaeus (120–202 CE). It is important to point out that Irenaeus did not develop a theodicy himself. Rather his writings provide the intellectual scaffolding upon which Hick built his response to the problem of evil.[24] Whereas the free will theory relies on an Augustinian notion of fallenness, an Irenaean one does not.[25] As Hick writes:

> Irenaeus suggests that man was created as an imperfect, immature creature who was to undergo moral development and growth and finally be brought to the perfection intended for him by his Maker. Instead of the fall of Adam being presented, as in the Augustinian tradition, as an utterly malignant and catastrophic event, completely disrupting God's plan, Irenaeus pictures it as something that occurred in the childhood of the race, an understandable lapse due to weakness and immaturity rather than an adult crime full of malice and pregnant with perpetual guilt.[26]

This theodicy hinges on a belief in the creation of humanity in two distinct steps. As Hick writes in his essay "An Irenean Theodicy," in this first stage, human beings were produced in the "image" of God, in a very slow, gradual evolutionary process.[27] People were created originally as spiritually and morally immature beings, which leads to the second stage of human creation. The second phase, which continues today, is one in which human beings are, through their own free will, ushered into what Irenaeus called

23. Ibid., 84–85.

24. Some, including theologian Mark S. M. Scott, argue that Hick at times misappropriates Irenaeus's writings, selectively choosing what supports his argument and ignoring other parts of his work that don't. For more see chapter 4 of Scott's *Pathways in Theodicy*.

25. Hick, "Irenean Theodicy," 39–40.

26. Hick, *Evil and the God of Love*, 220–21.

27. Hick, "Irenean Theodicy," 40.

the divine "likeness" of God.[28] This is an evolutionary view of creation, in which an ideal state of perfection is a slow and ongoing process only to be fully realized at the time of the eschaton. While humanity continue (and individuals in particular continue) to make moral progress, there is also an accretion of evil. As Hick writes:

> Man is in the process of becoming the perfected being whom God is seeking to create. However, this is not taking place—it is important to add—by a natural and inevitable evolution, but through a haphazard adventure in individual freedom. Because this is a pilgrimage within the life of each individual, rather than a racial evolution, the progressive fulfillment of God's purpose does not entail any corresponding progressive improvement in the moral state of the world. There is no doubt a development in man's ethical situation from generation to generation through the building of individual choices into public institutions, but this involves an accumulation of evil as well as of good.[29]

Unlike Augustine, Ireneaeus posited that humanity was not originally created in an idealized state of perfection, in direct contact and union with God. Rather, humanity was intentionally created at a distance from God. This kind of distance is not spatial but rather epistemic. Hick argues that only through this distance could finite human beings truly exercise genuine freedom. As he states, "One has space to exist as a finite being, a space created by this epistemic distance from God and protected by one's basic cognitive freedom, one's freedom to open or close oneself to the dawning awareness of God that is experienced naturally by a religious animal."[30]

Hick believes, relying on Irenaean thought, that human beings are created in this way so that they may come to know God in a genuinely free way. Hick argues that no rational being, created in full and unmitigated contact with God, would choose to do anything that is contrary to his divine will. He goes on to posit that while a creature originally created in the state of moral perfection would in theory be free to sin, it stands to reason that this creature would never choose to do so. As he states, "a responsible free being does not act randomly, but on the basis of moral nature, and a free being whose nature is wholly and unqualifiedly good will accordingly

---

28. Ibid., 41.

29. Hick, *Evil and the God of Love*, 292.

30. Hick, "Irenean Theodicy," 42.

never in fact sin."[31] Thus, Hick concludes that humans had to be created in this type of epistemic distance from God.

Hick relates moral evil to the fact that human beings are born in this separated state from God, and their moral perfection is emerging slowly through an evolutionary process. These early humans were "the raw material for a further and more difficult stage of God's work."[32] In its primitive beginnings human survival depended upon killing animals and other humans whose interests conflicted with their own. Humankind, created slowly apart from God, has always been and continues to be morally imperfect. For Hick, the core of moral evil is selfishness. He defines selfishness as the tendency to put one's own needs before the needs of others and to use others as a means of ensuring one's own survival.[33] Thus, seen through this evolutionary lens, moral evil is the result of the primal and animalistic nature of humanity that has been expressed throughout the ages. As Hick describes it, "this basic self-regardingness has been expressed over the centuries both in sins of individual selfishness and in the much more massive sins of corporate selfishness, institutionalized in slavery, exploitation, and all the many and complex forms of social injustice."[34] Despite this simple animal nature, God is slowly and gradually creating morally perfect creatures. The final creation of humanity will come when individuals freely respond to God's loving call, overcoming their own sinful and selfish nature. As Hick summarizes in *Evil and the God of Love*, people "may eventually become the perfected persons whom the New Testament calls 'children of God' but they cannot be created ready-made at this."[35]

In addressing natural evil, Hick argues that this type of suffering also results from the aforementioned human evolutionary process. In addition, his model is similar to free will theodicy's assertion that human intellectual development depends on interacting with a natural world, which functions according to its own objective laws. As Hick writes, "in a world which lacked a stable nexus of natural law that inflicts pain upon individuals and extinction upon species that are not adapted to its demands, the evolutionary

31. Ibid., 43.
32. Hick, *Evil and the God of Love*, 290.
33. Hick, "Irenean Theodicy," 44.
34. Ibid., 45.
35. Hick, *Evil and the God of Love*, 291.

process would scarcely have progressed beyond its earliest stages, and the world would probably still be inhabited mainly by jellyfish."[36]

Hick believes this type of environment is also an important component in human moral development. He is clear in affirming that the development of the whole person—intellectual, spiritual, moral, and so forth—is the "product of challenge and response that could not occur in a static situation demanding no exertion and no choices."[37] He defines a morally wrong act as one that in some way damages the human community whereas the morally right act is one that prevents or minimizes human harm. A natural world without suffering, pain, disease, or the like would be one where no moral choices would be necessary. As Hick argues, in this kind of world "There would be nothing wrong with stealing, because no one could ever lose anything by it . . . and in short none of the terms connoting modes of injury—such as cruelty, treachery, deceit, neglect, assault, injustice, unfaithfulness—would retain its meaning . . . It would be a world without need for the virtues of self-sacrifice, care for others, devotion to the public good, courage, perseverance, skill, or honesty."[38] Thus, no action would ever be morally wrong because no action would ever have harmful consequences.[39] Hick posits that God created humanity in a world full of these dangers and uncertainties because it is only in such a world that mutual caring and concern can ever be elicited.[40]

Hick believes that life on this earth is intended to be one of soul-making. The maximization of pleasure and avoidance of pain is not God's main goal for humanity. To illustrate this point, Hick analogizes the parenting by what he sees as good and wise parents with God's desire for his creation:

> We have to recognize that the presence of pleasure and the absence of pain cannot be the supreme and overriding end for which the world exists. Rather, this must be a place of soul-making. And its value is to be judged, not primarily by the quantity of pleasure and pain occurring in it at any particular moment, but by its fitness for its primary purpose, the purpose of soul-making.[41]

36. Ibid., 342.
37. Hick, "Irenean Theodicy," 46.
38. Hick, *Evil and the God of Love,* 361.
39. Hick, "Irenean Theodicy," 46–48.
40. Ibid., 50.
41. Hick, *Evil and the God of Love,* 295.

Thus, some suffering can be seen as beneficial in playing a role in the soul-making. However, Hick acknowledges that gratuitous evil cannot be adequately addressed by his theodicy, at least as lived in this life on earth. As he puts it, "so far as we can see, the soul-making process does in fact fail in our own world at least as often as it succeeds."[42]

As a result, a crucial component of Hick's theodicy is its eschatological rootedness. In fact, without it, he asserts that one cannot refute the claims of critics like Mackie, who argue that the existence of evil proves that God cannot be both all-powerful and all-loving. Hick writes that his theodicy must look beyond this life

> towards the future, expecting a triumphant resolution in the eventual perfect fulfillment of God's good purpose . . . we must thus affirm in faith that there will in the final accounting be no personal life that is unperfected and no suffering that does not eventually become a phase in the fulfillment of God's good purpose. Only so, I suggest, is it possible to believe in the perfect goodness of God and in His unlimited capacity to perform His will. For if there are finally wasted lives and finally unredeemed sufferings, either God is not perfect in love or He is not sovereign in rule over His creation.[43]

This soul-making process, one in which individuals overcome their own selfish impulses to respond to the needs of others, is not one that can ever fully be completed on this earth. In fact, it continues in some kind of purgative state, or put in less Catholic terms, one of "progressive sanctification."[44] Eventually, the human soul is ultimately fulfilled, and at that time all evil, even gratuitous suffering that seemingly produces no good effect, is rendered worthwhile.[45]

42. Ibid., 372.
43. Ibid., 376.
44. Ibid., 384.
45. Ibid., 377.

Process Theodicy

In order to properly understand process theodicy[46] some background information is needed.[47] Process theology, and resulting theodicy, is rooted in the philosophy of Alfred North Whitehead (1860–1947).[48] The fundamental tenet of a process worldview is that reality is ultimately composed of dynamic energy events rather than completed objects or substances. Whitehead's system is called process because all things are in constant state of becoming. He believes that for anything to be actual, it must be in the process of its own becoming, or an ingredient in the becoming of something else. In contrast to the worldview inherited from the Greeks, Whitehead asserts that "to be" is "to become," and that a thing's becoming constitutes its essence. As he writes, "how an actual entity becomes constitutes what that actual entity is; so that the two descriptions of an actual entity are not independent. Its 'being' is constituted by its 'becoming.' This is the 'principle of process.'"[49] Whitehead also held that the basic "things" in the universe are not thing-like. That is, instead of these "things" being thought of as enduring substances, they are momentary events. Whitehead writes, "Thus the actual world is built up of actual occasions; and by the ontological principle whatever things there are in any sense of 'existence,' are derived by abstraction from actual occasions. I shall use the term 'event' in the more general sense of a nexus of actual occasions, inter-related in some determinate fashion in one extensive quantum. An actual occasion is the limiting type of an event with only one member."[50]

Whitehead insists that each event is also self-creative. By that he means that each event determines its own becoming by the way it experiences itself in relation to its environment. This does not mean that every event in the universe exercises a conscious, deliberate choice to become one thing rather than another. Instead Whitehead argues that the actual existence of

46. Inclusion of this theory is necessary because it is one of the prominent contemporary responses to the problem of evil. However, it should be noted that while Merton was familiar with Whitehead's work, process theodicy was not developed until after Merton's death. Therefore it had no influence on his own thoughts about the problem of evil.

47. I do not attempt to explore all of the nuances of process thought in this section. Instead, the goal is to provide a satisfactory, if not broad, overview.

48. Scholars have noted the Buddhist influence on Whitehead and its similarities to process thought. For more on this topic see Inada, "The Metaphysics of Buddhist Experience." In chapter 4 the Zen and Buddhist influence on Merton will be examined in depth.

49. Whitehead, *Process and Reality*, 23.

50. Ibid., 73.

that event is determined by its own experience of itself, not by another entity outside of it. "The functioning of one actual entity in the self-creation of another actual entity is the 'objectification' of the former for the latter actual entity. The functioning of an eternal object in the self-creation of an actual entity is the 'ingression' of the eternal object in the actual entity."[51] In addition, one ramification of this type of philosophy is that there is not a stark difference between humanity and other creatures and parts of the universe. Instead there is a spectrum of evolutionary progress, from the molecule to the human, with increasing levels of freedom.[52]

Process theologian David Ray Griffin first developed process theodicy and dealt with it comprehensively in his 1976 book, *God, Evil, and Power*. Given the complexity of this theory, Griffin continues to address and refine it in books and essays.[53] Griffin begins presenting his theory by challenging the orthodox belief that God created the universe out of nothing, i.e., *creatio ex nihilo*. He points to contemporary biblical scholarship to support his argument that the creation account in the book of Genesis should be interpreted and understood as God creating the universe out of chaos, not out of nothing. This distinction will play a key role in his theodicy.[54]

The difference between creation out of chaos and creation out of nothing is an important one for Griffin. He argues that creation out of chaos suggests that the material, or chaos, from which our universe was created had some kind of power of its own. Therefore, there are parts or elements of the universe that would not all wholly be subject to God's will. Griffin argues that it then follows that human beings have some power not directly under God's power. Seen this way, when surveying history Griffin argues that one should not expect it to consistently reflect God's divine will. He states that if one affirms the traditional concept that God created out of nothing, then examples of gratuitous evil and suffering, such as the Holocaust, must be seen as being a part of God's divine plan.[55] Griffin builds on this idea of God's limited power in constructing his theodicy.

---

51. Ibid., 23.

52. Griffin, "Creation Out of Nothing," 120.

53. See Griffin's books, *Evil Revisited*; and *Panentheism* and *Scientific Naturalism: Rethinking Evil, Morality, Religious Experience, Religious Pluralism, and the Academic Study of Religion*, as well as the essay "Creation Out of Nothing, Creation out of Chaos, and the Problem of Evil."

54. Griffin, "Creation of out Nothing," 108.

55. Ibid., 108–9.

Griffin stresses the importance of this concept of shared power in describing his theodicy. While God is the highest or supreme example of power and creativity in the universe, he is not the only embodiment of these traits. Therefore, and importantly for his theodicy, God does not have a monopoly on power. Human beings, who are at the high end of the evolutionary spectrum, have developed a great deal of freedom, and therefore God cannot summarily take it away or override it.[56] As Griffin explains:

> Accordingly, it is impossible for God to have a monopoly on power. There must be an actual world; and every actual world will necessarily contain actualities with power—some power of self-determination, and some power to influence others. This twofold inherent power provides the twofold reason why God cannot unilaterally effect any state of affairs in the world that is intrinsically possible. God cannot totally determine the concrescence[57] of any actual occasion: (1) since that occasion will necessarily be partly determined by previous actual occasions, which themselves could not have been totally determined by God; and (2) since the present occasion necessarily has some power to create itself, beyond all the influence of others, including God.[58]

The significant implication of this idea of shared power is that God can only persuade, not coerce. Griffin is clear to say that God is always persuading his creation towards good moral choices. Therefore, God provides an "initial aim," but each "actual occasion" then supplies its subjective aim, once again demonstrating God's restricted, persuasive power.[59] Put differently, God supplies the best moral choice in a situation, but each individual is free to make his or her own decision.

Given that within this process framework God cannot coerce a human being to actually make those morally preferred choices, Griffin argues that God is not to blame for evil and suffering in the world. Since God does not

---

56. Ibid., 122.

57. By way of explanation, Griffin states that individuals are momentary events that happen and then end, making way for succeeding events. These are also defined as "actual occasions." Each of these actual occasions exists in two modes: "first one and then the other. An occasion comes into being as an experiencing subject. The data of its experience are provided by previous actual occasions. Its reception of these data is called its 'feelings' or 'positive prehensions' of those previous occasions . . . It becomes a unified subject by integrating these feelings. This process of integration into a concrete unity is called 'concrescence'" (God, Power, and Evil, 277).

58. Griffin, God, Power, and Evil, 279–80.

59. Ibid., 280–81.

have a monopoly on power and can only persuade and not coerce, he cannot be blamed for evil and suffering.[60] This applies to suffering caused by both moral and natural evils. Griffin believes his process theodicy is much more preferable to those that posit that God has the power to unilaterally prevent gratuitous evil and suffering yet fails to do so.[61]

Cruciform Theodicy

The last Christian approach to the problem of evil to be examined is cruciform theodicy. This theory is rooted in the notion of divine passibility, which is the belief that God is not detached from the joys and suffering of his creation. Rather, "God suffers with, from, and for humanity on the cross of Christ. The doctrine hinges on divine love and argues that love entails suffering, since the object of love—humanity—suffers."[62] This is contrary to the long held belief that God is unaffected by human feelings. Theology of divine passibility began in Europe after the First World War, when many were trying to make sense of the brutality of mechanized war along with the anxiety caused by the Industrial Revolution. This movement was propelled even further, decades later, by the gratuitous and unthinkable atrocities of the Holocaust. Those seeking to make sense of these events began to point to the suffering of Christ, where the incarnate God joins fully with human suffering, as a model of divine love. That is, of a love that suffers. "God suffers because he loves. God's vulnerability arises from God's emotional investment in creation as the creator. True love suffers, it does not stand aloof."[63] Many found this kind of deity, a God who suffers with humanity, preferable to a detached, impassible one. Finally, theologian Jürgen Moltmann's influential 1972 work, *The Crucified God*, popularized the case for God's passibility.

Philosopher and Episcopal priest Marilyn McCord Adams has teased out implications of God's passibility for the problem of evil. Adams posits that the Christian belief in God's incarnation, and redemptive suffering on the cross, provides a useful way to approach the problem of evil. As she writes, "My bold contention will be the Christian approach to evil through

---

60. Griffin, "Creation out of Nothing," 122.

61. Ibid., 109.

62. Scott, *Pathways in Theodicy*, 152.

63. Ibid., 153.

redemptive suffering affords a distinctive solution to the problem of evil."[64] Adams affirms that Christ's suffering on the cross transforms human suffering, making it spiritually redemptive. Further, God's incarnation in Christ and suffering creates an existential and spiritual link between divine and human suffering, and places all human suffering within the context of Christ's redemptive suffering. As a result, Adams affirms that when humanity suffers, we experience God. As she writes, "so perhaps our experiences of deepest pain as much as those of boundless joy are themselves direct (if still imperfect) views into the inner life of God. Further, just as lesser joys and pleasures (for example the beauty of nature, music or art) may be more obscure visions of the glory of God, so also lesser degrees of suffering."[65]

In addition, Adams points to the tradition of Christian martyrs as a model for how redemptive suffering can occur here and now. Adams defines a martyr as "someone who gives testimony about a person, some events, or an ideal and who is made to pay a price for doing it."[66]

The act of martyrdom can provide redemptive use for the onlooker, the persecutor, and even the martyr herself. For the onlooker, the martyr's principled sacrifice can serve as a powerful example, a prophetic story to shape that witness's life. In addition, the onlooker may see elements of herself in the attitudes and acts of the one persecuting the martyr, and in this realization may be moved to repentance.[67] Similarly, the sacrifice of the martyr can have a positive impact on the persecutor. Seeing the martyr's sacrifice up close can serve as a stark contrast to her own life, thus leading to deeper insights about the state of her own life. In addition, Adams argues that, "the cross of Christ is the chief expression of God's love for the persecutor. If the persecutor is moved to repentance by the love of the martyr, it is the martyr whom he will thank and love."[68] Further, Adams asserts that the experience can be positive and redemptive for the martyr as well. If the martyr's loyalty to God remains strong after being tested, the relationship with God, the crucified Christ, is strengthened and deepened. As she writes, "The religious martyr who perseveres at the cost of his life wins the highest good. For in loving God more than any temporal good and trusting God to see to his good in the face of death, he is rightly related to God. He

64. Adams, "Redemptive Suffering," 170.

65. Ibid., 184.

66. Ibid., 177.

67. Ibid., 177–78.

68. Ibid., 179–80.

is also freed from the power of evil, because evil controls us only by bribing us with temporal goods we want more than we want to obey God. There is no remaining capital with which to "buy off" the martyr who is willing to pay the highest price for his loyalty.[69] Finally, Adams uses this martyrdom model to address the problem of natural evil, writing, "much suffering comes through natural causes—disease, natural disaster, or death—and so apparently involves no personal persecutor (other than God) who can be moved to repentance by the victim's plight. Here, nevertheless, the victim's faith in God may be tried and emerge stronger."[70]

While Adams tries to show that redemptive suffering is possible during this lifetime, she is clear to emphasize that the main thrust of her theodicy is eschatological. Adams, a believer in universal salvation,[71] argues that union with God after death, participating in the beatific vision, will make all suffering, even those varieties that are excessive and fail to produce any recognizable good here in this life, finally redeemed. As she writes:

> The good of beatific, face-to-face intimacy with God is simply incommensurate with any merely non-transcendent goods or ills a person might experience. Thus, the good of beatific face-to-face intimacy with God would engulf . . . even the horrendous evils human experience in this present life here below, and overcome any prima-facie reasons the individual had to doubt whether his/her life would or could be worth living.[72]

Thus cruciform theodicy holds that in the end even the most egregious evils will be outweighed by God's goodness.

Evil and Suffering in Zen

As will be thoroughly discussed in chapter 4, Merton was heavily influenced by Zen Buddhism in the last several years of his life. Specifically, he gained most of his knowledge of Zen through the writings of D. T. Suzuki. It is therefore appropriate to examine some Zen approaches to the problem of evil. Suzuki understood Zen to be a form of Buddhism that did not have any specific philosophy of its own, except what is accepted by the Buddhists

69. Ibid., 181.

70. Ibid., 181.

71. Adams, "Afterword," 200.

72. Adams, "Horrendous Evils and the Goodness of God," 218.

of the Mahayana school.[73] Therefore it is useful to note that the Buddha taught that the cause of suffering is desire, which is rooted in ignorance. That is to say that it is ignorance of the interrelatedness of being, and failure to appreciate the impermanence of all things. Ignorance of these truths about reality leads to continued suffering, for when people act in their own selfish interests, they are in effect going against the grain of the universe, are running after and away from things that do not exist. Therefore, suffering is the unavoidable result. In addition, attachment to things inevitably leads to sorrow because joys associated with them will all be fleeting because of their impermanent nature. According to the Mahayana and Zen traditions, we are born into a world in which we think dualistically. When we discriminate this from that, we alienate ourselves from the truth, which is found when one overcomes dualism. So those two traditions affirm that language is inadequate to help one answer life's ultimate questions, because language is itself dualistic. These concepts are explored in more depth in chapter 4.

Suzuki affirmed a belief that suffering can have a beneficial impact on one's character. As he writes, "For the more you suffer the deeper grows your character, and with the deepening of your character you read the more penetratingly into the secrets of life. All great artists, all great religious leaders, and all great social reformers have come out of the intensest [sic] struggles which they fought bravely, quite frequently in tears and with bleeding hearts. Unless you eat your bread in sorrow, you cannot taste of real life."[74]

In addition, Suzuki also espoused a belief in the transmigration of the soul. It should be noted that the existence of a soul, that contains one's immortal essence and transmigrates is not a standard Buddhist view, and seems to be at odds with the standard Buddhist doctrine of nonself, or *anatman*.[75] Suzuki's belief in the transmigration of the soul relates to the notion of karma—the belief that beings are reborn according to the nature and quality of their past actions. In this way creatures can be thought to be the heirs to their intentional actions. All intentional actions, good or bad, leave a trace on the psyche that will determine the kind of existence into which the being will be reborn.[76] As Buddhist scholar Peter Harvey writes, "What determines the nature of a karmic 'seed' is the will or inten-

---

73. Suzuki, *Studies in Zen*, 57.

74. Suzuki, *Essays in Zen Buddhism (First Series)*, 16.

75. For more see Harvey, *Introduction to Buddhism*, 61–62.

76. Ibid., 39.

tion behind an act . . . It is the psychological impulse behind an action that is 'karma', that which sets going a chain of causes culminating in a karmic fruit. So if someone says of some event in their life 'it's my karma', a more accurate use of Buddhist terminology would be to say 'it's the result of my karma.'"[77]

Suzuki clearly affirmed a belief in karma as a response to the problem of evil. The following long quote from his writing illustrates this belief in karmic rebirth. He states:

> The idea of transmigration is this: After death, the soul migrates from one body to another, celestial, human, animal, or vegetative.
>
> In Buddhism, as it is popularly understood, what regulates transmigration is ethical retribution. Those who behave properly go to heaven, or to heavens, as there are many heavens according to Buddhist cosmology. Some may be reborn among their own races. Those, however, who have not conducted themselves according to moral precepts will be consigned after death to the underground worlds called Naraka.
>
> There are some destined to be reborn as a dog or a cat or a hog or a cow or some other animal, according to deeds which can be characterized as pre-eminently in correspondence with those natures generally ascribed to those particular animals. For instance, the hog is popularly thought to be greedy and filthy . . . Sometimes we are said to be born as plants and even rocks.
>
> The interesting thing about this idea of transmigration as sometimes told by Buddhists is that we do not stay in heaven or hell forever. When our karma is exhausted, we come out of hell or come down from heaven. Even when we turn into cats or dogs, we do not repeat this kind of life all the time. We may be reborn as human beings again if we do something good while living as a lower animal, though it is highly doubtful that, for instance, the cat can be taught not to steal fish from the neighbors—which is what she does quite frequently in Japan—however well she may be fed at home. But so far nobody has advanced the method of calculating mathematically the strength of karma according to the character of each deed. Therefore, we can never tell how long our life in heaven or hell will be. In any case, we know this much: there is a time when we have to leave heaven or hell.[78]

77. Ibid., 40.
78. Suzuki, *Mysticism*, 51.

Suzuki acknowledges that this belief is not readily provable by science. However, he writes that he is personally inspired by the idea, "and as to its scientific and philosophical implications, I leave it to the study of the reader."[79]

Another Zen take on the problem of evil is addressed by Zen's attempt to overcome dualism.[80] This call to move beyond dualism impacts how evil is perceived. Vietnamese Zen monk Thich Nhat Hanh has written about this subject. While Suzuki was Merton's main source of Zen knowledge, Merton was also very familiar with Nhat Hanh's work. The two were contemporaries and exchanged correspondence, and in fact, in 1966 they met when Nhat Hanh visited Merton's monastery. Finally, Merton wrote in support of Nhat Hanh's opposition to the Vietnam War in an essay titled "Thich Nhat Hanh Is My Brother." In addressing the problem of evil, Nhat Hanh posits that too many people are consumed with the dualistic difference between good and evil. He argues this occurs when people forget that good is also made of nongood elements. He illustrates this point with the following analogy:

> Suppose I am holding a lovely branch. When we look at it with a nondiscriminating mind, we see this wonderful branch. But as soon as we distinguish that one end is the left and the other end is the right, we get into trouble. We may say we want only the left, and we do not want the right . . . and there is trouble right away. If the rightist is not there, how can you be a leftist? Let us say that I do not want the right end of this branch, that I only want the left. So, I break off half of this reality and throw it away. But as soon as I throw the unwanted half away, the end that remains becomes the new right. Because, as soon as the left is there, the right must be there also. If I become frustrated, and do it again, breaking what remains of my branch in half, I will still have a right and left.[81]

Thus, Thich Nhat Hanh asserts that one cannot be, or have, the good alone. He argues that Western theology and philosophy have struggled to resolve the problem of evil. He proposes that when viewed through the prism of nonduality, there is in fact no problem. As he writes, "As soon as the idea of good is there, the idea of evil is there . . . You need both right and left in order to have a branch. Do not take sides. If you take sides, you

---

79. Ibid., 55.

80. Zen's drive to overcome dualism will be discussed in chapter 4.

81. Hanh, *Heart of Understanding*, 30.

are trying to eliminate half of reality, which is impossible."[82] In addition, Buddhist scholar and philosopher Masao Abe echoes this very point, asserting that good and evil are dependent on each other, and one cannot exist without the other. There is no absolute or supreme good, or evil, and to Buddhists "the supreme good and absolute evil are illusions."[83]

It is also important to point out some basic differences between the Christian and Zen approaches to the problem of evil. Although the Zen and Buddhist tradition do offer responses to evil and suffering, there is no explicit theodicy. There is no notion of God; therefore there is no need to reconcile a belief in a benevolent and all-powerful deity with evil and suffering in the world.[84] In addition, the Christian approaches clearly differentiate between good and evil, always with a call for good to ultimately prevail. As I have already noted, the Zen approach asserts that good and evil are indispensably connected.

Another difference between the two approaches has to do with the notion of intentionality. While theodicies from the Christian tradition categorize suffering that results from natural disasters, illness, and the like as natural evils, the Zen framework has no corresponding notion. As I discussed above, within Buddhist tradition, only an act's intention can be good or evil. Suffering therefore is not considered in any way to be an evil in and of itself; suffering can be the result of evil intentions.

Summary and Conclusion

The intent of this chapter is to provide an adequate summary of modern Christian responses to the problem of evil, as well as a brief examination of two approaches found in Zen thought. First, all of these responses either explicitly or implicitly point to the possibility of a positive or redemptive use for suffering. Free will and soul-making theodicies relate moral evil to bad human acts, and affirm that natural evil results from a world in which God limits direct interaction in human affairs. Cruciform theodicy does not attempt to explain the cause of evil or why God allows it, and instead focuses on what God does about it. Process theodicy attacks the problem in

---

82. Ibid., 31.

83. Abe, "Problem of Evil in Christianity and Buddhism," 145.

84. Whereas Buddhism has no corresponding belief in an all-powerful God, it does feature a variety of gods and other divine beings. For more see Harvey, *Introduction to Buddhism*, 33–36.

a unique way, positing that God is unable to coerce humanity and prevent suffering caused by bad human acts. Finally, Zen approaches to this problem affirm the positive results that suffering can produce. In addition, D. T. Suzuki points to the notion of the transmigration of the soul to explain individual suffering as the result of past bad acts. On the other hand, Thich Nhat Hanh points to the need to overcome the dualist distinction between good and evil, and accept that they are both necessary parts of the whole.

It is important to underscore that many may find that no theodicy satisfactorily addresses the problem of evil. As free will theodician Stephen T. Davis asks, are any theodicies "credible when trying to account for the Holocaust?"[85] In addition, it is doubtful that someone dealing with a personal tragedy would be comforted by any of these approaches. However, by recognizing the limitations and true goals of theodicy, one can better appreciate its proper role. A good theodicy is one that provides a path for approaching the problem of evil. It should not be thought of as a way to discover a definitive or conclusive answer to it. Despite their inherent limitations, theodicies still maintain a vitally important role. A theodicy can serve as a valuable guide for the faithful to further explore the mystery of how evil and suffering exist in a universe created and inhabited by an all-powerful, all-loving God.

Finally, theodicy remains an important endeavor because suffering is truly universal and timeless. One only needs to look at the last hundred years of human history to see a staggering litany of appalling human acts and natural disasters. In addition, each human life bears the indelible mark of personal suffering. Both global and individual suffering demand that a theist ask, why? Theodicy is meant to help guide that questioner.

Thomas Merton did indeed espouse a particular response to the problem of evil. It was consistently expressed for over two decades, but at the end of his life it began to change significantly. To properly identify and define it, one must look at his entire body of work and piece together his thoughts about the subject as they are revealed over the decades. That project is the undertaking of the next chapter.

85. Davis, "Introduction," xiii.

3

Thomas Merton's Theodicy (1938–1963)

Thomas Merton never set out to write a systematic treatise about the problem of evil. Therefore he did not devote a book, an article, or even a large
portion of his writing to the subject. However, a careful review of his entire
body of work reveals that Merton returned again and again to the subject.
While he often only visited this topic fleetingly, and with no regularity, it
is, however, possible to discover what type of theodicy he espoused. In this
chapter I trace the development of Merton's theodicy, built up bit by bit
over decades, and make the following arguments: First, by examining all
the various threads of this topic found in Merton's writings, one can as-
semble a consistent line of thought evident throughout his adult life about
the topic of evil and suffering. Second, Merton espoused what I am calling
a purified soul theodicy for most of his life. This is evident after examining
a wide range of his corpus (e.g., books, published letters, journals, and lectures given at conferences). The first pillar of this theodicy is that suffering
purifies the human soul. The second pillar of this theodicy is that while
Merton writes in some instances that God permits evil, in many others he
states that God causes suffering to bring about a particular good. In addition, Merton at times espoused elements of a cruciform theodicy, careful to
emphasize that God never abandons us, and joins with us when we suffer.

Before exploring Merton's own work, we must build a contextual
foundation by examining a few central concepts that influence a theodicy.
Specifically, it is necessary to broadly explore Merton's theological approach

and then move on to his conception of evil. Then it is important to examine his notion of original sin and fallenness, as those concepts play a crucial role in Christian theology. Once this is accomplished, we can examine his writings to identify his theodicy and how it developed and evolved over the course of his life.

It must be noted at the beginning of this project that whereas Merton often wrote about theological topics, he did not consider himself a theologian or a philosopher. As he was known to tell a host of correspondents, "I am a poet rather than a theologian."[1] In addition, as a monk he was greatly shaped by a particular kind of Christian theology: monastic theology. Jean Leclercq, a monk, scholar, and contemporary of Merton masterfully presented the unique characteristics of monastic theology in his book *The Love of Learning and the Desire for God: A Study of Monastic Culture*, and it serves as the primary source for the following excursus.

Monastic theology emerged as a reaction to the scholastic theology in the twelfth century. Scholastic theology, taught in the town schools of Europe, sought to apply reason in an effort to attain as much clarity on issues as possible. In many ways it endeavored to demystify God. Monastic theology developed in reaction to that perceived degradation of mystery. It is important to point out that monastic theology was not anti-intellectual. Knowledge was always preferable to ignorance.[2] As the famous twelfth-century Cistercian monk Bernard of Clairvaux wrote, "Again, how shall a shepherd who is without learning lead forth the flock of the Lord safely into the pastures of the divine Scriptures?"[3]

Monastic theology was leery about a tendency in scholastic theology that did not respect the mystery of God. Scholastic theology was often seen as an attempt to crack open the mystery of God, to "penetrate it as if by forcible entry after breaking the seal of mystery."[4] In writing about the Eucharist in the twelfth century, Bernard of Clairvaux, proponent of monastic theology, encapsulates this ideal by stating, "This sacrament is great; it must be venerated, not scrutinized."[5] While scholastic theology

---

1. Merton, *Hidden Ground of Love,* 330.

2. Leclercq, *Love of Learning and the Desire for God,* 193–202.

3. Bernard, of Clairvaux, *Sermons on the Canticle of Canticles,* Kindle Location 10290.

4. Leclercq, *Love of Learning and the Desire for God,* 204.

5. Ibid., 204.

very often employed the thought of philosophers as a resource, monastic theology relied more heavily on scripture.[6] As Bernard of Clairvaux wrote:

> But let us, my brethren, proceeding with simplicity and caution in this exposition of a sacred and mystical utterance, accommodate ourselves to the usage of Holy Scripture, which, in our human words, "speaketh wisdom hidden in a mystery"; which, commends the Divinity to our love by investing Him with human affections; and which, from the familiar images of earthly objects, as from chalices of vile material, gives our human minds to drink things rare and precious, even the mysterious and invisible.[7]

The effort of theology within the monastery was to seek a kind of higher knowledge about God that was a complement to faith. Ultimately it was seen as an important part of this union of God along with prayer and contemplation.[8] This was preferred to the more rational efforts of the scholastic school.

The theology developed in the monasteries was one in which reason and intelligence drew primarily from the content of faith itself. As monk and scholar Jean Leclercq describes, "Instead of proceeding by rational conclusions and demonstrative reasoning, it questions, in order to understand one aspect of God's mysteries, all other aspects as revealed in Christian sources."[9] In addition, while scholastic theology often responded to controversies and issues that would periodically arise, monastic theology was much less apt to do so, content to keep its focus on the meaningful search for and union with God.[10]

As this part of the chapter ends, I must raise two important points. First, while differences did indeed exist between scholastic theology and monastic theology, one should not conclude that their divergence constituted two completely different, unrecognizable approaches. Rather, they should be seen as two schools of one Christian theology, each with its own emphasis. Second, and pertinent to the study of Thomas Merton, monastic theology is not a relic of the Middle Ages. It still plays an important part in the theological formation and orientation of monks today. As Leclercq puts

---

6. Ibid., 223.

7. Bernard, of Clairvaux, *Sermons on the Canticle of Canticles*, Kindle Locations 9862–65.

8. Leclercq, *Love of Learning and the Desire for God*, 214.

9. Ibid., 215.

10. Ibid., 224.

it, "Monastic theology no more belongs to the life of the past than does the theology of the Fathers. It is not a stage which is now over, and its role is not ended."[11] Thomas Merton's formation as a monk was influenced by this theological approach. This kind of theological training and orientation also helps explain why Merton never attempted to systematically address the problem of evil. It is within this context that one can begin to explore Merton's understanding of evil and how he thought it fit into God's divine plan.

It is important to examine Merton's basic understanding of evil. This is key in order to then explore the way he believes it is used by God. This is not intended to be an exhaustive treatment on the varieties and kinds of evil Merton described throughout his life: e.g., war, racism, totalitarianism, and so forth. Rather it is an attempt to attain a basic understanding of how he understands the nature of evil, how it came into the world, and so on. Merton believes evil is not something that was created by God. Rather, it is a privation of the good. Plato and Augustine of Hippo (345–430) also espoused this conception of evil, and it was clearly adopted by Merton. Writing as early as 1939, two years before he entered the monastery, Merton explicitly defines evil in an Augustinian sense: "Saint Augustine's problems are everybody's, except he did not have a war to worry him. The 12th Chapter of Book VII [of Augustine's *Confessions*] is magnificent. Evil the deficiency of good. Everything that is, is good, by virtue of its mere existence."[12] This conception of evil is one he repeatedly used over the years. In his 1948 best-selling autobiography *The Seven Storey Mountain*, Merton writes, "Since evil is the defect of good, the lack of a good that ought to be there, and nothing positive in itself, it follows that the greatest evil is found where the highest good has been corrupted."[13] This definition appears again in 1962 when Merton writes, "Evil is not a positive entity but the absence of a perfection that ought to be there. Sin as such is essentially boring because it is the lack of something that could appeal to our wills and our minds."[14] Although influenced by a variety of theologians, Merton was an unabashed admirer of Augustine. As he enthused, "The light of God shines to me more serenely through the wide open windows of Augustine than through any other theologian. Augustine is the calmest and clearest light."[15]

11. Ibid.

12. Merton, *Run to the Mountain*, 3.

13. Merton, *Seven Storey Mountain*, 57.

14. Merton, *New Seeds of Contemplation*, 128.

15. Merton, *Entering the Silence*, 388.

Given Merton's reliance on this notion of evil, it is worthwhile to briefly examine Augustine's position. Writing in *The City of God*, Augustine describes that evil was not a separately created entity, made by God. Rather, it occurs when some part of God's creation abuses its free will. As he writes:

> The true Light, which lighteth every man that cometh into the world—this Light lighteth also every pure angel, that he may be light not in himself, but in God; from whom if an angel turn away, he becomes impure, as are all those who are called unclean spirits, and are no longer light in the Lord, but darkness in themselves, being deprived of the participation of Light eternal. For evil has no positive nature; but the loss of good has received the name "evil."[16]

Augustine affirms that everything that is created by God is in fact good. In *On the Nature of Good* he again explicitly states, "When accordingly it is inquired, whence is evil, it must first be inquired, what is evil, which is nothing else than corruption, either of the measure, or the form, or the order, that belong to nature. Nature therefore which has been corrupted, is called evil, for assuredly when incorrupt it is good; but even when corrupt, so far as it is nature it is good, so far as it is corrupted it is evil."[17]

Finally, an important aspect of this conception of evil is the notion that it has a parasitic relationship to the good. That is to say that since it is a corruption of the good, it could not exist on its own and is therefore dependent on the goodness of creation. The following quote from Augustine illustrates this point:

> But although no one can doubt that good and evil are contraries, not only can they exist at the same time, but evil cannot exist without good, or in anything that is not good. Good, however, can exist without evil. For a man or an angel can exist without being wicked; but nothing can be wicked except a man or an angel: and so far as he is a man or an angel, he is good; so far as he is wicked, he is an evil. And these two contraries are so far co-existent, that if good did not exist in what is evil, neither could evil exist; because corruption could not have either a place to dwell in, or a source to spring from, if there were nothing that could be corrupted; and nothing can be corrupted except what is good, for corruption is nothing else but the destruction of good. From what is good, then,

---

16. Augustine, *City of God*, 269.

17. Augustine, *On the Nature of Good*, Kindle Locations 46–49.

evils arose, and except in what is good they do not exist; nor was there any other source from which any evil nature could arise.[18]

It is clear then that Merton had an Augustinian notion of evil. That is to say that evil was not a metaphysical entity that God created. Rather, moral evil results when creatures with free will turn away from God. When this occurs, the good nature of human creation is corrupted, and this corruption is what is defined as "evil." Further, seen in this way evil is wholly dependent on the goodness of creation and continues to exist in this parasitic way.

In addition, Merton believed in the notion of original sin and the fallenness of humanity. His thoughts about original sin are important to understand as that notion influences his understanding of evil and suffering. The following is a brief summary of these concepts.

Merton writes often about the notion of original sin and the human state of fallenness. In many of his writings he explicitly refers to the biblical account of Adam and Eve's banishment from the garden of Eden—the result of humankind's fall from a state of perfect union with God. Although he subscribed to this belief in an Adamic fall, Merton read and understood this portion of the Genesis story in a figurative way. In fact Merton did not espouse a fundamentalist view of Scripture. He makes that view of Scripture clear in his writings. He explicitly addressed this when he wrote, "The early chapters of Genesis (far from being a pseudo-scientific account of the way the world was supposed to have come into being) are precisely a poetic and symbolic revelation, a completely true, though not literal, revelation of God's view of the universe and of His intentions for man."[19] In addition he also writes about the way that Scripture and science are complements to each other. In his only published novel, originally written before he entered the monastery but reworked and sent to the publisher shortly before his death, Merton speaks through one of his characters on this subject. Mrs. Frobisher, a woman whom the community looks to for wisdom and advice, says the following:

> "No one has ever found the missing link between man and the ape," Mrs. Frobisher continued, "and yet science knows evolution is true. But since religion knows the Bible is true, how can science be true and religion be true?" It was a question that had never bothered me, but it was a question. "It is all perfectly simple," she

18. Augustine, *The Enchiridion*, Kindle Locations 840–48.

19. Merton, *New Seeds of Contemplation*, 296–97.

said. "The Book of Genesis merely says in a symbol the same thing that the theory of evolution says in science. The seven days of Genesis are more than likely a symbol for seven hundred thousand or maybe seven million years, I forget which.

"Yet in the Book of Genesis, which means the creation, the creatures are made in the same order science says they were, starting with the lowest and ending with the highest of all. And there really isn't any conflict at all between Darwin and the Bible: the Bible is the symbol of Darwin's theory, and Darwin's theory is the scientific way of saying how they were all created."[20]

This understanding of how Merton read Scripture is important to note so that his writings on the notion of original sin and human fallenness can be properly understood as related to a general state of human estrangement from God rather than as punishment for our primogenitors' eating of forbidden fruit.

Merton believed that human beings are born into sinful societies that promote our alienation from one another, and more important, from our true selves. That for Merton was original sin. He succinctly expresses this belief when he writes:

To say I was born in sin is to say I came into the world with a false self. I was born in a mask. I came into existence under a sign of contradiction, being someone that I was never intended to be and therefore a denial of what I am supposed to be. And thus I came into existence and nonexistence at the same time because from the very start I was something that I was not. To say the same thing without paradox: as long as I am no longer anybody else than the thing that was born of my mother, I am so far short of being the person I ought to be that I might as well not exist at all. In fact, it were better for me that I had not been born.[21]

In addition, Merton develops this point and explicitly defines this idea of original sin in a 1959 letter to Zen scholar D. T. Suzuki. Merton writes:

Then comes the question whether or not the Resurrection of Christ shows that we had never really been separated from Him in the first place. Was it only that we thought we were separated from Him? But that thought was a conviction so great and so strong that it amounted to separation. It was a thought that each one of

20. Merton, *My Argument with the Gestapo*, Kindle Locations 821–29.
21. Merton, *New Seeds of Contemplation*, 35–36.

us had to be God in his own right. Each one of us began to slave and struggle to make himself a God, which he imagined he was supposed to be. Each one slaved in the service of his own idol— his consciously fabricated social self. Each one then pushed all the others away from himself, and down, beneath himself: or tried to. This is Original Sin. In this sense, Original Sin and paradise are directly opposed. In this sense there is exclusion from paradise. But yet we are in paradise and once we break free from the false image, we find ourselves what we are: and we are "in Christ."[22]

In these two passages one can see Merton's belief that original sin was not some kind of metaphysical stain on the human soul relating to a literal Adam and Eve's expulsion from the garden of Eden. Rather, Merton understood original sin to be a state of alienation and estrangement, both from our true selves and from God, into which we are born.

Merton and the Purified Soul Theodicy

Period One: 1938–1949

As I have already been stated, Merton was not a philosopher or theologian. In addition, although he wrote prodigiously, he did not devote any books or articles to the problem of evil. It is only by carefully examining a wide selection of writings (e.g., published journals, letters and books) and using the hermeneutical lens of theodicy that one can see that Merton did in fact espouse a particular response to the problem of evil. As I will show, it is one that would develop over time. This material can be explored in a variety of ways, but I believe progressing chronologically through Merton's work is the best approach. If we move chronologically, we will see the evolution of Merton's thought. A chronological examination of his thought on the problem of evil will give us opportunities to focus on themes related to this topic—themes that captured Merton's interest throughout his life.

Merton himself grouped his writings into three distinct periods. The first begins with his conversion to Catholicism in 1938 and continues through 1949. As he describes this monastic phase of time, "I was totally isolated from all outside influences and was largely working with what I had accumulated before entering. [I drew] on the experience of the monastic life in my early days when I was quite ascetic, "first fervor" stuff,

---

22. Merton, *Hidden Ground of Love*, 564.

and when the life at Gethsemani was very strict. This resulted in a highly unworldly, ascetical, intransigent, somewhat apocalyptic outlook. Rigid, arbitrary separation between God and the world, etc."[23] The second period is the longest and runs from 1950 through 1963. This was a time, as Merton describes it, "when I began to open up again to the world, began reading psychoanalysis (Fromm, Horney, etc.), Zen Buddhism, existentialism and other things like that, also more literature. But the fruits of this did not really begin to appear until the third period."[24] Finally the third period starts roughly in 1964 and runs through the end of his life in December 1968. Merton describes this era by writing, "It appears that I am now evolving further, with studies on Zen and a new kind of experimental creative drive in prose poetry, satire, etc."[25] With this in mind I now focus on his first period to show how he believed evil and suffering fit into God's divine plan.

In Merton's earliest writings he begins to develop the idea that God allows and at times even causes suffering for the betterment of humanity. This idea first appears in his personal journals that he kept before entering the monastery. In 1940 he wrote:

> However, to say that God is punishing the Church is far worse than imagining that He ought, right now, at our wish, to punish the Nazis. God does not punish the Church: He punishes sinners—and how He does we cannot very well conceive. Wars, plagues, famines have something to do with His punishment, not so much because they are the punishment itself, but because they are warnings of the eternal punishment to come.[26]

Even in this early passage Merton espouses the belief that God takes an active hand in causing suffering towards a particular end. Writing less than a year later, he states that God allows suffering: "The Savior permits suffering, to punish certain sins, to test the fidelity of those who love Him, and to give man an opportunity to help others. The sufferings are never so great that a person cannot bear them or must be unhappy, if he has the Savior with him."[27]

Around this same time Merton also began to include references to what would be a minor theme in his writings about evil and suffering: i.e.,

---

23. Merton, *School of Charity*, 384.

24. Ibid.

25. Ibid.

26. Merton, *Run to the Mountain*, 222.

27. Ibid., 285.

elements of a cruciform theodicy. As I noted in chapter 2, cruciform theodicy is the belief that through Christ's crucifixion God suffers with and for us. It is God's identification with human suffering in the incarnation that enables our identification and participation with Christ in our suffering. This incarnate suffering creates an existential and spiritual link between Christ's suffering and ours, "a cosmic compatibility that situates individual experiences of horror within the salvific framework of Christ's redemption. When we suffer, we experience God, if we suffer in solidarity with him, and that allows the integration of these experiences into our lives."[28]

In a journal entry from May 1940 Merton gestures towards this kind of cruciform theodicy by showing Christ's solidarity with those who suffer. As he writes, "For Christ suffers in the Church: and there is nothing suffered on earth that Christ Himself does not suffer. Everything that happens to the poor, the meek, the desolate, the mourners, the despised, happens to Christ."[29] Merton firmly believed that God never abandons us.

In returning to the main elements of Merton's theodicy in the first period, in 1947, a year before his autobiography *The Seven Storey Mountain* was published, Merton first wrote about his belief that God uses suffering for the purification of the human soul. His superiors, recognizing his talents as a writer, asked him to write a history of Mother Berchmans, an early twentieth-century Cistercian nun who left her convent in France to help revive a struggling foundation in Japan. In chronicling her life and its various trials and tribulations, Merton first began expressing this idea that God causes suffering in order to purify the soul. As he first writes, "And therefore the trials that are calculated to purify us the most are precisely the ones which escape the capacity of our own understanding and which flatly contradict the most fundamental tendencies of our own will."[30] In this next passage Merton explicitly states that God causes suffering as means to a specific end. As he writes in *Exile Ends in Glory*:

> For when God tries us, and means us to have a real, inescapable, and empirical knowledge of our nothingness, he even teaches us, beforehand, all the truths we might need to think our way out of our temptations, if thinking could possibly save us: and then he

28. Scott, *Pathways in Theodicy*, 171.

29. Merton, *Run to the Mountain*, 223.

30. Merton, *Exile Ends in Glory*, x.

allows us to suffer all the more from our complete inability to put into effect what we have seemed to know and understand.[31]

Within this same book Merton continues building on that theme by quoting a fellow monk. Here he more explicitly turns toward the idea that suffering is used by God to destroy one's existing identity so that it can be purified. Merton writes:

> The whole doctrine is admirably summed up in the journal of one of our great modern Cistercians, Dom Symphorien . . . He writes "Where God is leading us is not to sanctity as it is too commonly understood, that is to say, the embellishment of ourselves: but to annihilation and destruction of ourselves. But, if we are to attain this end, God will have to do everything: select our crosses, place them on our shoulders, pick us up after our falls, strip us, nail us, make us die on the cross: the hand of the Lord alone can do all this!"[32]

In addition, Merton's journals again provide valuable insights into his thoughts on this matter. In the spring of 1948 Merton recorded the following gruesome local plane crash in his journal:

> One very sad thing: a plane crashed in our woods yesterday afternoon about two o'clock. Six people all killed, terribly mangled, bodies cut to pieces and then burned—a woman's hand up in a tree—two children in the wreck. They were going somewhere for Easter, just getting near Louisville. What a terrible Easter for some family, or two families! I hope the reason God let them crash here at this time was to give them a part in our prayers.[33]

This is an especially noteworthy entry. Merton kept regular journals throughout most of his life. In them he chronicled everything from news items, mundane details of the monastic life as well as profound insights about a host of topics. This passage is important because of its casual nature. By casual I mean that there is no indication that Merton picked up his journal on that date to record his thoughts that could lead to an article or book chapter on why humans suffer. Instead, he is chronicling the day's events and mentions this horrific incident, briefly commenting on it. Its value here is that this passage's casual nature bespeaks his deeply held belief

31. Ibid., 62.

32. Ibid., 63.

33. Merton, *Entering the Silence*, 199.

about human suffering. The reflexive, almost stream-of-consciousness character of a journal entry demonstrates Merton's belief that God allows suffering, "let them crash," in order to bring about a particular good.

In 1948 Merton was asked to write another hagiography, this time about the life of Cistercian mystic and nun Saint Lutgarde of Aywieres. In this work Merton turns again to this notion that God allows and in some cases causes suffering in order to purify the human soul. Here he is the most explicit in making this argument as he is in any of his past writings. It appears primarily in two passages. First, he writes:

> It is consoling to learn that even the greatest mystics are purified by much the same trials and anxieties and temptations and perplexities as ordinary monks and nuns: but it should be more than merely consoling. Ought we not perhaps to conclude that if God tries us in the same fire, it is because He would like to bring us to the same purity, and give us the same rewards?[34]

Merton is clearly arguing that God is actively involved in causing these "trials and anxieties," and that they are used to purify. In this next passage Merton is even more explicit in making these points. As he states:

> Not content with this, the infinite purity of God attacks the soul with the blind pain of His immediate presence-which causes fierce torture to the soul full of impurities and imperfections. In this way, God is ruthlessly burning out every stain, every slightest relish in the soul: but the helpless and blinded victim sees nothing but the horror of its imperfection, and feels nothing but the furious attack of this force which it has no means of identifying or comprehending, except to know that it comes from God's infinite justice.[35]

As we will see in the next chapter, Merton's thoughts on how evil and suffering fit into God's divine plan evolved. However, at this point Merton had arrived at a position that would fundamentally be his main one until a few years before his death.

Merton continued to build on this theme in the next year and would also introduce another theme that he would devote a great deal of time to exploring. Merton writes about individuals being separated from their true selves. As will be explored later, he blames this on a number of factors. What is of particular interest here is that Merton continues to touch upon

---

34. Merton, *What Are These Wounds?*, 46–47.

35. Ibid., 50.

the topic of suffering and how God uses it to purify the soul. In the following passage from his 1949 book *Seeds of Contemplation* he uses a new metaphor to make that point. As he writes:

> Souls are like wax waiting for a seal. By themselves they have no special identity. Their destiny is to be softened and prepared in this life, by God's will, to receive, after death, the seal of their own degree of likeness to God in Christ. And this is what it means, among other things, to be judged by Christ. Therefore if you spend your life trying to escape from the heat of the fire that is meant to soften and prepare you to become your true self, and if you try to keep your substance from melting in the fire—as if your true identity were to be hard wax—the seal will fall upon you at last and crush you. You will not be able to take your own true name and countenance, and you will be destroyed by the event that was meant to be your fulfillment.[36]

Merton uses this metaphor to express his belief that God actively causes suffering that one encounters in life, or "the heat of the fire" for the betterment of the human soul.

Correspondence during this period also shows that Merton believed that God allowed and sometimes caused suffering for specific ends. In a 1949 letter he wrote to a nun, to be used for a class she was teaching, Merton states, "The evil that is in the world is the punishment of the sins and passions of men who have lived easy and luxurious and sinful lives and have taught everybody else to believe that everything consists in having pleasure and satisfying all their passions."[37] Here Merton is clearly stating that the abuse of free will causes sin. In addition, he also implicates God, as evil is the "punishment" that God causes.

Finally, during this period Merton begins to comment on the book of Job. It is a topic that he would touch upon throughout his life when pondering the notion of evil and suffering. This book of Hebrew and Christian Scripture (of the Old Testament) tells the tale of a prosperous and just man, Job, whom God chooses to test. God sends him a series of trials that include the loss of his fortune, the deaths of loved ones, and painful illnesses. Despite these misfortunes, Job remains faithful to God and does not blame him. His friends visit Job to grieve and help him make sense of his adversity. Each tells him essentially the same thing: that God is just, and therefore

36. Merton, *Seeds of Contemplation*, 98.
37. Merton, *Road to Joy*, 321.

Job must have done something to earn this punishment. He rejects their opinions and continues to question why the innocent suffer and the wicked prosper. God finally reveals himself to Job and describes the breadth and complexity of his creation in order to demonstrate that Job and the rest of humanity are simply incapable of understanding God. Job responds by admitting that there is no way for him to understand the mind, or question the motives, of an infinite God.

Merton's first writing about the book of Job is found in his journal in the fall of 1949. As will be seen, Merton continues to affirm the notion that God causes suffering, and explicitly states that God uses suffering to purify humanity. As he writes:

> It is alarming to find out how much one's theology fits the theology of Job's friends! The form of the drama of Job demands that the reader identify himself with Job. Actually most of us are more like Eliphaz or Baldad. We are hardly much closer to God than they were. And, after all, at least one of them was a mystic. Eliphaz started out with a modest enough explanation of Job's suffering, based on mystical experience. I am startled to find that this is the interpretation I myself made of Job eight years ago . . . *Numquid homo, Dei comparatione, Justificabitur? aut factore suo purior erit vir?* "Shall man be justified in comparison with God, or shall a man be more pure than his maker [Job 4:17]?" And the same strain is taken up by Baldad in XXV, 4 [*Numquid justificari potest homo comparatus Deo?*] Then, too, *Beatus homo qui corripitur a Deo* (Job 5:17), "Blessed is the man whom God correcteth" is written on the heart of every Trappist in the first months of his novitiate. God's purity, says Eliphaz, who knows from experience, causes us anguish and suffering when we come in contact with Him. But it is for our good that He thus purifies us.[38]

Here Merton not only reveals his thoughts about the book of Job, but in the passage above also shows his continued belief that God intends for suffering to "purify us." In ruminating further about this book of Scripture, Merton emphasizes that the faithful should follow Job's example and not seek answers as to why God chooses to purify our souls through suffering in the way he does. As Merton writes:

> We should be humble and patient. Which reminds me that Job is a proverbial model of patience when he was anything but patient: at least so his friends thought. But that is only one of the

38. Merton, *Entering the Silence*, 369.

paradoxes of Job. His tempestuous impatience is really a higher form of patience. It is a kind of adoration. Really, the problem of Job is not so much to find out who has the right answer to the question of suffering. All their answers are more or less correct. But what Job himself demands, and justly, is the Divine answer, not to the problem of suffering in general, but to his own personal suffering. In the end, the answer that God gives to Job is simply a concrete statement of what Eliphaz has said in the abstract: "Shall man be compared to God?" Job wanted the answer and he got it. God Himself was his answer. In the presence of God, Job acknowledged his sufferings to be just and God reproved all the arguments of Job's friends, because they were all insufficient.[39]

Finally, Merton concludes by stating that the book of Job holds no universal answer to the problem of evil. As he puts it,

> Thus the Book of Job does not solve the problem of suffering, in the abstract. It shows us that one man, Job, received a concrete answer to the problem, and that answer was found in God Himself. If we are to have Job's answer, we must have Job's vision of God. Otherwise, our arguments are only modifications of the arguments of Job's friends. I hasten to say that those arguments should be sufficient for most of us. But they probably would not have been sufficient for Job.[40]

As has been stated, Merton returns to the book of Job throughout his life. His writing about it at this point reinforces the assertion that Merton very much believed God allowed, and in some cases caused suffering to purify the human soul.

Period 2: 1950 through 1963

This second period is the longest of Merton's life as a writer and monk. Spanning more than a decade, the period saw his continued interest in the topics of evil and suffering. Interestingly, this period also saw Merton's writings about the Second World War and more specifically the Holocaust. Given the relevance of these events to the problem of evil, we will explore what Merton had to say about them.

39. Ibid.
40. Ibid.

Merton continued to address the issue of suffering during this time, even if somewhat sporadically. In 1953 Merton published a version of his journals for the first time, *The Sign of Jonas*, and in it he returns to the topic of Job. His thoughts about Job and suffering in this published journal are essentially like the ones already discussed above, found in his private journal entry from 1949. In both versions Merton explicitly states that God intends for suffering to purify humanity.[41] This similarity is important to note because it reaffirms the fact that his original thoughts about Job, recorded informally in his journal of 1949, indeed represented Merton's thought-out position about the book of Job and suffering. His 1949 entry was more than fleeting. That the passage survived the selection and editing processes and was included in a book to be published and widely read demonstrates that Merton did indeed come to his ideas about Job and suffering after considerable reflection.

In his 1953 book *Bread in the Wilderness* Merton begins by describing a photo of a crucifix. It depicts "the Christ Who shares His agony with the mystics. And finally it is the Christ of our own time—the Christ of the bombed city and of the concentration camp."[42] This certainly relates to his earlier comments that describe a cruciform theodicy that unites Christ with those that suffer. Here again Merton clearly shows his belief that God never abandons us, even when we suffer.

Writing in 1955 Merton again expresses the idea that God allows suffering for the betterment of humanity. In addition, he also points to the human abuse of free will as the root cause of suffering. "The Lord did not create suffering. Pain and death came into the world with the fall of man. But after man had chosen suffering in preference to the joys of union with God, the Lord turned suffering itself into a way by which man could come to the perfect knowledge of God."[43] In this same work Merton explicitly makes the point that sometimes God causes suffering: "Neither the beginning of suffering is important nor its ending. Neither the source of suffering is important nor its explanation, provided it be God's will."[44]

Again in the same work Merton deals with the issue of suffering by incorporating elements of a cruciform theodicy. The following passage illustrates the idea that humanity enters into solidarity with God through

41. Merton, *Sign of Jonas*, 234–35.
42. Merton, *Bread in the Wilderness*, 1.
43. Merton, *No Man Is an Island*, 89.
44. Ibid., 90.

our suffering as well as the eschatological hope of entering into the kingdom of God. Merton writes, "We all live together in the power of His death which overcame death. We neither suffer alone nor conquer alone nor go off into eternity alone. In Him we are inseparable: therefore, we are free to be fruitfully alone whenever we please, because wherever we go, whatever we suffer, whatever happens to us, we are united with those we love in Him because we are united with Him."[45]

In returning to his purified soul theodicy, Merton next addressed the book of Job with a brief journal entry in the fall of 1957: "No easy generalizations about Job and Zen. Job is a big koan. So is everything else."[46] While this one line is not compelling on its own, it is noteworthy for two reasons. First, it supports the argument that while he did not dedicate a specific work to the problem of evil, indeed a line of thought addressing the topic runs throughout his writing. Second, this passage gestures towards a point that will be argued in more depth in the next chapter: Merton's immersion in Zen had an increasing influence on how he approached the world, including evil and suffering.

During this time, when teaching the novice monks, Merton also conveyed the belief that God at times causes suffering for particular reasons. His prepared notes for these sessions clearly exhibit this when he wrote, "God wants us to suffer because perfection is attained only through suffering. Then too, by suffering we undergo punishment which is rightly meted out upon a world in which, generally speaking, men do not devote themselves to duty."[47]

In addition, Merton continues to espouse this belief that God is active in causing suffering for a particular end in his correspondence during this period as well. In 1961 he wrote a letter to Grayson Kirk, the president of Columbia University. In it he explicitly makes the point that God uses suffering as a means of purification: "Hence we must purify our hearts and our faith, seeking the will of God not in a negative resignation only, but with every hope that He may show us some positive way of action that can counteract the forces that are inexorably advancing against the Church. No doubt His way will be to purify the Church by suffering and persecution."[48] In addition, in a 1962 letter to a longtime correspondent, Merton writes "I

45. Ibid., 86–87.
46. Merton, *Search for Solitude*, 116.
47. Merton, *Life of Vows*, 54.
48. Merton, *Witness to Freedom*, 77.

am glad that light and liberation have come into your life, with the Holy Spirit. Do not be surprised however if he also sometimes brings darkness and crisis. Crisis is both necessary and fruitful and the religious view of life makes crisis more fruitful, and truly so."[49]

During this period Merton also addressed the evil of Nazism. The Holocaust, and its systematic attempt to exterminate the Jews, serves as the seemingly insurmountable modern hurdle for any theodicy to adequately address. It is important then to examine Merton's thoughts about it during these years. I do not attempt here to address all of Merton's writings about Nazism, the Holocaust, or Second World War. Instead, I focus on correspondence in which the topic of the problem of evil was broadly addressed, as well as Merton's writing about infamous Nazi Adolf Eichmann.

In 1958 Merton began a decade long series of correspondence with Polish writer and poet Czeslaw Milosz. Merton initiated the relationship, writing to Milosz after reading his study of the social psychology of Communism, *The Captive Mind*.[50] Milosz, who had survived the Nazi occupation of Warsaw and Stalinist rule of Poland, shared with Merton a recognition that the modern evils of "totalitarianism, scientism, atomic war, and racism were among the greatest threats to mankind's ability to sustain belief in a just God and in Providence."[51] As a result, questions of evil, suffering, and God's role in them appeared in their letters. An exchange in the late spring of 1959 features the most direct treatment of this subject. In a May 1959 letter Milosz questions the notion of God's providence in light of the Nazi death camps.[52] Merton's response, while long, is important to examine.

> As for Providence: certainly I think the glib clichés that are made about the will of God are enough to make anyone lose faith. Such clichés are still possible in America but I don't see how they can survive in Europe, at least for anyone who has seen a concentration camp. For my part, I have given up my compulsive need to answer such questions neatly. It is safer and cleaner to remain inarticulate, and does more honor to God. I think the reason why we cannot see Providence at work in our world is that it is much too simple. Our notions of Providence are too complicated and too human: a question of ends and means, and why this means to this end? God wills this for this purpose . . . Whatever the mystery of Providence

49. Merton, *Hidden Ground of Love*, 110.

50. Faggen, *Striving towards Being*, vi.

51. Ibid., v.

52. Ibid., 22.

may be I think it is more direct and more brutal in a way. But that is never evident as long as we think of God apart from the people in concentration camp, permitting them to be there for their own good (time out while I vomit).[53]

Here Merton's thought echoes many others in admitting that the immense evil of the Holocaust makes any theodicy seem inadequate. He concedes that it is impossible to understand how the Holocaust could be a part of God's plan, yet he does not deny that it somehow is. In addition, his statement that "I have given up my compulsive need to answer such questions neatly" will be shown to be false, as he repeatedly returns to his purified soul theodicy over the next several years.

In the next portion of this same response to Milosz, he espouses elements of a cruciform theodicy by affirming that Christ shares the suffering of his creation. Merton continues:

> Actually it is God himself who is in the concentration camp. That is, of course, it is Christ. Not in the collective sense, but especially in the defilement and destruction of each individual soul, there is the renewal of the Crucifixion. This of course is familiar, I mean the words are familiar. People understand them to mean that a man in a concentration camp who remembers to renew his morning offering suffers like and even, in some juridical sense, with Christ. But the point is whether he renews the morning offering or not, or whether he is a sinner, he is Christ. That this is not understood even by religious people: that it cannot be comprehended by the others, and that the last one to be able to understand it, so to speak, is "Christ" Himself . . . Providence is not for this hidden Christ. He Himself is His own Providence. In us. Insofar as we are Christ, we are our own Providence.[54]

In this portion of his letter Merton affirms his belief that through his crucifixion, Christ is inextricably joined to every element of the human condition, not the least of which is suffering. In this next and last portion of Merton's response to Milosz he once again gestures towards a cruciform theodicy:

> The thing is then not to struggle to work out the "laws" of a mysterious force alien to us and utterly outside us, but come to terms with what is inmost in our own selves, the very depth of our own

53. Ibid., 38–39.
54. Ibid., 39.

being. No matter what our "Providence" may have in store for us on the surface of life (and this inner Providence is not really so directly concerned with the surface of life) what is within, inaccessible to the evil will of others, is always good unless we ourselves deliberately cut ourselves off from it. As for those who are too shattered to do anything about it one way or another, they are lifted, in pieces, into heaven and find themselves together there with no sense of how it might have been possible.[55]

This letter is one of the most direct responses Merton gives to how the Holocaust fits into God's will. While he acknowledges that humanity cannot really know why or how this could be a part of God's providence, he does affirm that it does. Merton also emphasizes that through the crucifixion Christ enters into all human suffering, and therefore God suffers with us. Finally, Merton is also clear to show that he does not believe the suffering of those in the death camps was "for their own good," and refrains from linking this evil and suffering to a greater good. However, in this correspondence he is ultimately clear in affirming that the Holocaust is somehow part of God's will.

In that same year Merton was also reading accounts of the Adolf Eichmann trial. The following passage, from his personal journal, is representative of his thoughts about Nazism and the Holocaust.

It's incredible, and shattering. The trial is not just an indictment of one man or one system, but is in fact a sordid examination of conscience of the entire west and one which has proved singularly inconclusive because no one seems to grasp anything definite about it (if they have even tried to grasp anything). All that remains is a general sense of loss, of horror and of disorientation. And even the horror is diffuse and superficial. Where does one begin to respond to the multiple indictments of our world? The stereotypical answers all collapse, and there are no new ones, and there is no faith![56]

This entry is emblematic of his writings about the Holocaust for two reasons. First, it shows that this evil was so gratuitous that it is difficult to fully comprehend. As has been mentioned, that idea was also present in the correspondence with poet Czeslaw Milosz. Second, Merton does not attempt to address it as an example of the problem of evil. In fact, in all of

55. Ibid., 39–40.
56. Merton, *Turning towards the World*, 306–7.

his writings about Nazis and the Holocaust, I have not found that Merton ever directly addressed how an all-loving and all-powerful God could allow this horrific evil to occur. At first blush it may seem odd that in all his writings Merton never attempts to explicitly answer that question. However, it is completely understandable if one reflects on what has already been presented as Merton's take on the problem of evil. Merton is careful to point out that, much like Job, he cannot comprehend the mind and motivations of an infinite God and why God operates as he does. However, the Holocaust, the embodiment of gratuitous evil in the twentieth century, was still part of God's overall schema. Merton does show in these writings that he believed it was very much part of God's will, produced some greater good, and contributed to purification of human souls.

The assassination of President Kennedy became a focal point for Merton's thoughts about how evil and suffering fit into God's divine plan. In two letters and a pair of presentations to fellow monks, Merton explicitly affirms, as much as he ever had, his belief that God allows and at times causes suffering for the betterment of humanity. The unpublished audio of a lecture[57] he gave to a group of novices on November 23, 1963, provides the clearest and most explicit example of his belief that God allows and in some cases causes suffering in order to produce a good. Merton begins his talk by giving the group the latest news that he's heard about the ongoing investigation into the president's death. He informs the monks that Lee Harvey Oswald had been arrested the day before and that he appears to be a "crackpot." Merton then says the following in what sounds like a matter-of-fact tone: that the president's assassination is "something that the lord has willed to have happen to our whole nation, and it's something we're all involved in and we have to pray over it, that's all." However, one of the novices quickly challenges Merton, and his premise that God actually willed the president's death. The following is my transcription of their fascinating discussion, in which Merton is clear that it was indeed God's will for this to happen:

Novice: He didn't will it did he? He permitted it.

Merton: He willed it. Do you have any doubt that this is God's will?

Novice: Well there are things he wills and things he permits.

57. Merton's lectures were recorded between April 27, 1962, and August 16, 1965, so they could be played for his fellow monks while they worked (Merton, *Life of the Vows*, xliv–xlvi).

72

Merton: Well what did he will in this thing and what did he permit?

Novice: Well the will has to permit it but—

Merton: Oh, see when you say, when you talk about the permissive will of God, what does God permit? What's the, why do you make this reservation about, he permits?

Novice: I would say he permits evil.

Merton: He permits evil. All right, now here what kind of evil do you have in this incident right here? You've got two kinds of evil. You've got a physical evil and you've got a moral evil. Which one does God will and which does he permit?

The novice says something indecipherable.

Merton: He permits moral evil, but everything else he wills. I mean physical evil he doesn't will as evil. But see, uh when a man pulls a trigger, and the bullet goes to its target, that's not permitted by God, that's willed by God. See, all these natural forces, and the natural operation of cause and effect, but what was permitted, uh and not willed, was the moral deordination on the part of the criminal. See, that's permitted, that's not willed. See the sin is permitted. But the effects of the sin are willed. See all of these things are part of, are willed. Not in the sense that God willed this individual to be shot, or anything like that, but because it forms part of a whole complex of causes and effects, all of which God willed. See, and all of which are for the best.

There are occasions in the above exchange in which Merton does state that God permits evil. However, he goes on to reinforce his belief that God was directly involved in this event by describing the difficult conditions of Oswald's shot that killed the president, and the unlikely, almost miraculous, nature of that bullet finding its target. As he describes, the difficulty involved in Oswald making that shot:

> See I'm talking about a still target at a hundred yards would be hard enough, but a moving target, at a hundred yards, in the middle of a whole lot of people, and when you're obviously not going to be totally calm, doing a thing like this you see, it's really uncanny that even a good shot could do that. Of course I've never shot with a telescopic lens but I know what it used to be like on a shooting range. We used to shoot at eighty and a hundred yards

and so forth and you have to raise your sights and all that sort of stuff. It's awfully hard to hit something at that distance.[58]

In addition, on this same date, Merton wrote a letter to Robert Kennedy's wife, Ethel Kennedy, to offer his prayers and condolences. Merton is again clear in asserting that God was actively involved in this event for particular ends:

> It is easy enough to say that this is the will of God. The question arises, precisely what is the will of God in this mysterious situation. It would be tautology to say that it was the will of God just because it happened. But to me the whole thing is so uncanny and so strange that I think we must see it as a warning once again to the whole country: it is in some sense a reminder that our moral condition is very hazardous, when the rights of a whole race are flagrantly violated, when those who attempt to do right and uphold justice are menaced and even killed. It means we must certainly pray and work hard for this country, to try and bring it through the critical times that do not seem to become any less tense as time goes on. I suppose we must resign ourselves to the task of living under special difficulties. May we be generous in doing so.[59]

Merton is clear that because of the "uncanny" and "strange" circumstances that one must see it as a warning from God.

Finally, less than a week later Merton wrote Jacqueline Kennedy. In this letter of November 27, 1963, he is less direct than he was in his lecture, and even in his letter to Ethel, in saying that God was active in causing this tragedy. One can easily see Merton taking a softer stance on the issue out of concerns for Mrs. Kennedy, rather than presenting his opinion in such a way as to call a grieving widow to grapple with the problem of evil. However, as the following passage shows, even in this letter Merton clearly sees God permitting the president's death to produce a good:

> The awful events of the past week have certainly been a kind of spiritual crisis for the whole nation, and a tragic, momentous, utterly mysterious expression out of something hidden in the whole world, that had to express itself as it has done, in evil and in good. I think it is beginning to be clear that God allowed this that He might bring great good out of it. You know what help He has given you, and given us all. You can surely hope that from this tragic and

58. Merton, *President's Death.*
59. Merton, *Hidden Ground of Love,* 447.

cruel explosion of irrationality and violence, clarity and reason can emerge.[60]

It is interesting to note that the tone and language of Merton's message during this week differs when speaking to the novices he is instructing, compared to the letters he wrote to a grieving relative and widow. Like any good writer, Merton knew his audience and played to it. He is explicitly clear when speaking to his students that the president's death was the will of God, and in fact took a novice to task when he tried to challenge that point. Yet, later that same day Merton wrote about God "permitting" this act and does not say that God willed it. Despite these differences, it is clear in the lecture to his fellow monks and letters he wrote to the family of President Kennedy that at this point in his life he still firmly espoused a belief that God allowed and in some cases caused suffering, as a part of his divine plan, and that it was used for the betterment of humanity.

Finally, on that same date, November 27, 1963, Merton gave another lecture to the novice monks. He once again updates the group about the latest news about Oswald's background.[61] He also states that after some additional reflection he can still see God's involvement in the president's death. The following is a transcript of the unpublished audio from that conference:

> Of course what this has really done, is actually, when you stop and look at the thing, it's really, in a sense you can see what God is doing out of it. First of all He is trying to wake everybody up. And secondly, it's the one way in which He has been able to bring home to people that what Kennedy was trying to do was serious. Because everybody has been fighting about it, and everybody has been against him. You know, I mean not everybody, but some for and some against and just general confusion, and now this fact of his having died in, in the thick of the thing, for following out his duty because he was trying to do what he believed in doing is going to

60. Ibid., 450.

61. Interestingly, Merton is prescient in his prediction that Jack Ruby's murder of Oswald would forever cast doubt as to who was truly responsible for the president's assassination. As Merton states, "The terrible thing is, this idiot who killed him, now they can't find out what happened. And nobody knows what happened. And the thing that's really bad about that is if, I mean until the end of time they'll be fighting about it, somebody will be saying that it was uh, I mean somebody will say it was Oswald that was really tied up with anybody they don't like and then the other people will say no it was Oswald that was up with these people; everybody is going to be hanging Oswald on somebody, and nobody will really know for sure," Merton St. Bernard's Apologia.

make people realize these things have to be done. I mean that it's really serious and very important. Maybe they'll believe him. So, very often they won't believe a person while he's alive, he has to die first. So, anyway let's pray it will come out like that.[62]

Merton is once again clearly showing his belief that God is using the president's death to produce a good.

Summary and Conclusion

Thomas Merton never set out to write a comprehensive, systematic treatise about the problem of evil. He did not consider himself to be a theologian in the formal sense, and was informed by a kind of monastic theology that sought truth and clarity while respecting the ultimate mystery of God. However, by using a wide lens and surveying Merton's work from beginning to this point in his life, it is possible to see that he did in fact espouse a particular kind of theodicy. First, Merton held an Augustinian view of evil in that it was not something created by God but rather resulted from a privation of the good. In addition, while he did not read the Bible in a literal way, Merton definitely believed humanity was in a state of fallenness, in which people are born into a world where they are often separated from their true selves, neighbor, and God. As a part of this notion of fallenness Merton believed that moral evil enters the world by the abuse of free will.

It is clear from his earliest writings that Merton believed that suffering was not only permitted but in some cases caused by God to produce a good. In addition, he consistently wrote that suffering leads to the purification of the human soul, thus I am using the term "purified soul theodicy." In as early as 1940 Merton's writings are illustrative of that belief. In fact, that thread of thought can be consistently traced through the next two and a half decades. He espouses this belief in correspondence, personal journal entries, lectures given to fellow religious, and books that he wrote. In addition, during this time Merton also exhibited his belief that God unites with us in our suffering. That is, a belief that though Christ's crucifixion God suffered with humanity, and humanity would ultimately be redeemed at the time of the eschaton. It is clear that Merton believed, whether it was a plane crash or president's assassination, that God allows and causes suffering here and now for the betterment of humanity.

---

62. Merton, *St. Bernard's Apologia.*

Interestingly, in the last few years of Merton's life his thoughts about the problem of evil began to change. While it's possible to find explicit examples of his purified soul theodicy as late as 1967, it is clear that in the last few years of his life Merton's thought on the subject was moving on a new trajectory. In the next chapter I examine his treatment of the problem of evil during this time and point to what may have been affecting this change.

4

Merton's Theodicy, 1964 through 1968, and His Changing Approach to the Problem of Evil

In the last period of Merton's life, he continued to address the problem of evil, and elements of his purified soul theodicy are still evident. However, as I will show, during this time his approach to the problem of evil is clearly changing. Specifically, one can see Merton abandoning the task of theodicy altogether. More and more in the period, when confronting the issue of God's role in human suffering, Merton simply refuses to pursue the task of theodicy. It is not the case that Merton's theodicy changed from one kind to another. Rather, he increasingly refused to try to give any explanation as to how and why suffering can exist in a universe with a God who is all-powerful and all-loving. I will argue that Merton's increased interest and immersion in Zen caused this change.

This last period of his life starts with Merton's continued affirmation of his purified soul theodicy. This is clearly seen in his 1965 book *Seasons of Celebration*. In the following passage he again returns to the theme that suffering purifies the human soul:

> The monastic vocation is a spiritual charism, a call to a life of consecration, trial, solitary combat, of obedience to the Holy Spirit in an eschatological battle between light and darkness. The monk too, baptized and sealed with the Spirit of Promise, imitates the Patriarchs, the Prophets, and Jesus Himself in a desert-life, renouncing the world of men, their concerns and their ambitions, not in order to affirm and perfect himself spiritually, but in order to serve God

by submitting to trial and purification, that his inmost freedom may be perfected in truth.[1]

Merton makes another mention in this work to God's purification when he writes, "Sin is pardoned, man is redeemed not by the destruction and punishment of man's freedom, but by its purification."[2]

Also around this time,[3] in the 1966 book *Conjectures of a Guilty Bystander*, Merton mentions evil and its causes. In describing the alienating tendency of technology he writes, "We no longer know how to live, and because we cannot accept life in its reality, life ceases to be a joy and becomes an affliction. And we even go so far as to blame God for it! The evil in the world is all our own making, and it proceeds entirely from our ruthless, senseless, wasteful, destructive, and suicidal neglect of our own being."[4] Here Merton reaffirms his long held belief that moral evil comes into the world because of the human abuse of free will. In particular, this passage shows that he believed that those things that distract us, or take us away from God, ultimately lead to alienation and unhappiness. As I have demonstrated though, while Merton traced the origin of moral evil to humanity's turning away from God, he also believed that God then allows and sometimes causes suffering to bring about a better good.

In fact, Merton makes that very point later in this work, discussing the suffering the Jews faced during the exodus: "I am struck and troubled by the fact that if the Jews were called out of Egypt, out of peace and into anguish, it was because God did not will that His People should merely live productive, quiet, joyous, and expansive lives."[5] Once again Merton affirms that God allows suffering.

Around this same time, in 1967, Merton wrote about the nature of suffering, with a particular emphasis on the benefits that should be sought from it.

1. Merton, *Seasons of Celebration*, 206–7.

2. Ibid., 218–19.

3. According to a letter written to psychologist Reza Arasteh (Merton, *Hidden Ground of Love,* 42), this passage was written in the fall of 1967 as a revised preface for the Japanese edition of his book *The New Man*. It was later published, along with other writings, in the 1979 book *Love and Living*.

4. Merton, *Conjectures of a Guilty Bystander*, 222.

5. Ibid., 314.

if the Christian "accepts" evil into his life with stoic indifference, or still worse remains unconcerned with the crises of society and of mankind, he cannot enter into communion with Christ.

"If he is to practice to the full perfection of Christianity, the Christian must not falter in his duty to resist evil." Why? Because evil is not something that God wills him to "undergo" with patience and negative resignation. God does not simply ask man to suffer. Suffering is an evil. If evil comes into our life, it is in order that we may grow and give glory to God by cooperating with him in resisting it. Christ's command "resist not evil" is no objection against this. On the contrary, the resistance forbidden by Christ is the simple, selfish instinct to repel suffering and to escape it. The Christian is bound to "overcome evil with good" and hence to resist it in a higher and more perfect sense: consciously and freely working to bring out of evil that good which is willed by God. Clearly this is a much more healthy and fruitful concept of Christian patience than the negative one which asks us to bear every stupid injustice, to obey and keep our mouths shut because, for some unknown reason which is none of our business, God has decreed that we must be crushed under some burden of suffering.[6]

Merton is once again clear here that God sometimes actively causes suffering; he declares, "God has decreed that we must be crushed under some burden of suffering." Here he also emphasizes the importance of facing suffering not just with passive resignation but rather with determination, in order to overcome it so that some good may result. In addition, Merton also points to his belief that God is with those who suffer and can provide strength in this fight.

Around this same time Merton wrote an article titled "The Death of God and the End of History," in which one can see elements of cruciform theodicy. He writes, "It is not that the world of Auschwitz, Vietnam and the Bomb has to be cursed and repudiated as the devil's own territory. That very world has to be accepted as the terrain of the triumph of love not in the condemnation of evil but in its forgiveness: and this is certainly not an easy truth when we confront the enormity of the evil!"[7] One can see this brief passage as reminiscent of a cruciform theodicy, in that Christ joins us in our suffering, identifies with the world, and redeems it through his crucifixion.

6. Merton, *Love and Living,* 180.
7. Merton, *Faith and Violence,* 258.

Merton and Camus

Merton's interest in Albert Camus provides valuable insights into his thoughts about the problem of evil, and how it changed during this last period of his life. Czeslaw Milosz urged Merton to read Camus.[8] Camus's writings had a tremendous impact on Merton, and in fact one biographer declares that "it would be hard to imagine the mature Thomas Merton without considering the full extent of Camus' influence."[9] In addition, as scholar David Belcastro points out, Milosz, Camus, and Merton all shared an interest in the condition of the modern world, but they commented from marginalized positions that each had taken within it.[10] Merton was so taken with Camus that he wrote seven essays about him between the years of 1966 and 1968. This is of particular relevance, as Merton addressed the problem of evil in writing about Camus. In particular, his comments about Camus's *The Plague* are especially informative.

The Plague, written in 1947, tells the story of an outbreak of disease that ravages the Algerian city of Oran. Merton read this story as Camus's critique of France and the French clergy during the Nazi occupation of the Second World War.[11] In *The Plague* Camus explores a variety of themes, including the suffering of the innocent and what he saw as the classic Augustinian Christian response to that subject.[12] As Merton writes, "*The Plague* is not only the physical epidemic but also the moral sickness of men under oppression by a hateful regime—a typological reign of evil."[13] In particular, the response to this crisis by one of its characters, Jesuit priest Père Paneloux, provides a direct foray into the topic of God's role in suffering.

It is worthwhile to briefly examine two parts of *The Plague* in order to better understand and appreciate Merton's commentary. First, Camus describes a fire-and-brimstone sermon given by Paneloux one month into

8. Faggen, *Striving towards Being*, 65.

9. Cooper, *Thomas Merton's Art of Denial*, 209. In addition, other biographers have also described Merton's affinity for Camus's work, including but not limited to Moses, *Divine Discontent*; Mott, *Seven Mountains*; and Horan, *Franciscan Heart*.

10. Belcastro, "Voices from the Desert," 107–8.

11. Merton, "Camus and the Church," 262.

12. Merton points out that "at the University of Algiers Camus wrote a thesis (1936) on early Christianity, Neoplatonism, Gnosticism, and St. Augustine. Camus attempted to explain the Augustinian attitude toward evil, which he found deeply repugnant, emphasizing the influence of Manichaeism and Neoplatonism" (Merton, *Literary Essays*, 184). For more about Augustine's concept of evil see chapter 3, above.

13. Merton, "*The Plague* of Albert Camus," 187.

the onset of plague. At this point in the story many have already died, and the city of Oran has been cut off from the rest of the world in an effort to contain the sickness. On a rainy Sunday morning that concluded a week of prayer for an end to the epidemic, Paneloux took to the pulpit and informed the overflowing cathedral that "calamity has come on you, my brethren, and, my brethren, you deserved it."[14] The scene continues:

> In strict logic what came next did not seem to follow from this dramatic opening. Only as the sermon proceeded did it become apparent to the congregation that, by a skillful oratorical device, Father Paneloux had launched at them, like a fisticuff, the gist of his whole discourse. After launching it he went on at once to quote a text from Exodus relating to the plague of Egypt, and said: "The first time this scourge appears in history, it was wielded to strike down the enemies of God. Pharaoh set himself up against the divine will, and the plague beat him to his knees. Thus from the dawn of recorded history the scourge of God has humbled the proud of heart and laid low those who hardened themselves against Him. Ponder this well, my friends, and fall on your knees."[15]

It is clear here that Camus's representative of Christianity in this book blames the victims of the plague as surely deserving the divine punishment they are receiving. One can't help but be reminded of the similar response Job's friends had, thinking Job must have done something to deserve the suffering that had befallen him. Paneloux continues this line of thought, declaring, "The just man need have no fear, but the evildoer has good cause to tremble. For plague is the flail of God and the world His threshing-floor, and implacably He will thresh out His harvest until the wheat is separated from the chaff. There will be more chaff than wheat, few chosen of the many called."[16] However, in the following two passages Paneloux's message takes on a Manichaean[17] edge when he says,

> Yet this calamity was not willed by God. Too long this world of ours has connived at evil, too long has it counted on the divine mercy, on God's forgiveness. Repentance was enough, men thought;

14. Camus, *The Plague*, 94.

15. Ibid., 94–95.

16. Ibid., 95.

17. Manichaeism relates to the teachings of Persian religious leader Mani (216–276 CE), who formulated a starkly dualistic religion in which there was a conflict between the force of good and of evil, light and dark. Before his conversion to Christianity Augustine was a follower. Collins and Farrugia, *New Dictionary of Theology*, 623.

nothing was forbidden. Everyone felt comfortably assured; when the day came, he would surely turn from his sins and repent. Pending that day, the easiest course was to surrender all along the line; divine compassion would do the rest. For a long while God gazed down on this town with eyes of compassion; but He grew weary of waiting, His eternal hope was too long deferred, and now He has turned His face away from us. And so, God's light withdrawn, we walk in darkness, in the thick darkness of this plague."[18]

In this final excerpt from Paneloux's sermon he more pointedly tells the congregation that

"My brothers," he cried, "that fatal hunt is up, and harrying our streets today. See him there, that angel of the pestilence, comely as Lucifer, shining like Evil's very self! He is hovering above your roofs with his great spear in his right hand, poised to strike, while his left hand is stretched toward one or other of your houses. Maybe at this very moment his finger is pointing to your door, the red spear crashing on its panels, and even now the plague is entering your home and settling down in your bedroom to await your return. Patient and watchful, ineluctable as the order of the scheme of things, it bides its time. No earthly power, nay, not even—mark me well—the vaunted might of human science can avail you to avert that hand once it is stretched toward you. And winnowed like corn on the blood-stained.[19]

In concluding, Paneloux explicitly states that God will produce good from this suffering of the plague:

It reveals the will of God in action, unfailingly transforming evil into good. And once again today it is leading us through the dark valley of fears and groans towards the holy silence, the well-spring of all life. This, my friends, is the vast consolation I would hold out to you, so that when you leave this house of God you will carry away with you not only words of wrath, but a message, too, of comfort for your hearts.[20]

In this sermon it seems clear that Camus is expressing three ideas. First, the suffering that is being endured is the direct result of those residents' sinful ways. In addition, God does not cause the suffering as much

18. Camus, *The Plague*, 95–96.

19. Ibid., 96–97.

20. Ibid., 99.

as he has turned his back on the city, washed his hands of the whole affair, and allowed the forces of evil to descend upon the community. In this way one can say God takes a less active, or passive, role, allowing it to happen. Finally, Paneloux affirms that God will indeed produce some good from this evil.

One other noteworthy episode in *The Plague* is worth exploring. It comes later in the story when the narrator, Dr. Bernard Rieux, and Paneloux are present when a child suffers an agonizing death, after taking an experimental dose of vaccine. Witnessing that, Rieux is understandably upset and Paneloux attempts to comfort him. The following is their brief exchange:

> "I understand," Paneloux said in a low voice. "That sort of thing is revolting because it passes our human understanding. But perhaps we should love what we cannot understand."
>
> Rieux straightened up slowly. He gazed at Paneloux, summoning to his gaze all the strength and fervor he could muster against his weariness. Then he shook his head.
>
> "No, Father. I've a very different idea of love. And until my dying day I shall refuse to love a scheme of things in which children are put to torture."[21]

It seems clear that through Dr. Rieux, Camus is rejecting the entire Christian response, as he understood it, to the problem of evil.

Now that Camus's material has been presented and briefly discussed, we can move forward with Merton's analysis of it, and specifically with what it has to say about how Merton understands, during this last period of his life, God's role in evil and suffering.

Analyzing this story and Paneloux's role, Merton affirms his belief that "the theme of the play as punishment for sin here echoes the preaching of many French Catholic priests and bishops after the fall of France during 'the great penitence of Vichy.'"[22] Examining Paneloux's sermon[23] above and the exchange with Rieux, Merton concludes that it is unappealing because of its overly didactic nature. He writes, "We must admit that his [Paneloux's] Christianity is defective. Why? Because one looks in vain for any evidence of a really deep human and Christian compassion in this

---

21. Ibid., 218.

22. Merton, "*The Plague* of Albert Camus," 188.

23. Paneloux gives a second sermon towards the end of the book where he softens his position.

stern, logical mind."[24] Merton goes on to say that Paneloux's God is not the God of Christian revelation and is "the perverse abstraction from centuries of futile argument."[25]

In another essay, "Terror and the Absurd: Violence and Nonviolence in Albert Camus," Merton uses Camus's writings as a rosetta stone for understanding horrific evils, such as the Holocaust. Merton states that in the times in which Camus was living—in this Death of God era—a vacuum was created in which humanity was drawn to ultimately feudal and potentially destructive ends.[26] Merton describes the Death of God movement as one that argues that historical religion and theology have not brought humanity closer to God. In fact, its proponents believe that these traditional approaches have failed and have in fact only alienated humanity further from any kind of meaning in the idea of God. As he puts it,

> To reject the Kingdom of God and of grace is to build a society on the abstract concept of 'justice' and this leads inexorably to the concentration camp . . . Note that this same logic operates not only in the death camps of a Hitler, labor camps of the Soviets or Red Chinese, but also where the power of unlimited destruction is concentrated in nuclear or other weapons.[27]

Again Merton does not attempt to address how the Holocaust can be reconciled with an all-loving, all-powerful God. Instead he points to it and other atrocities as being the inevitable outcomes of a world that is pointed towards humanity, and not God.

Merton's other writings about Camus, about the problem of evil, are of particular interest as I believe they exhibit the influence of Zen in the later part of his life. Merton's immersion in Zen, and its influence on how he

24. Merton, "*The Plague* of Albert Camus," 212.

25. Ibid., 213.

26. Merton describes the Death of God movement as one that argues historical religion and theology have not brought humanity closer to God. In fact, its proponents believe that these traditional approaches have failed and have in fact only alienated humanity further from any kind of meaning in the idea of God. As Merton puts it, "it is often mere sophomoric anti-religion and anti-clericalism, and seems to end by subjecting man more completely and more arbitrarily to the massive post-Christian secularism." ("Violence and the Death of God," 197.) For more about Merton's thoughts about the Death of God movement see the essays "Violence and the Death of God," "The Death of God and End of History," and "Godless Christianity?"—all in his book *Faith and Violence: Christian Teaching and Christian Practice.*

27. Merton, "Terror and the Absurd," 236.

responded to the problem of evil in the last years of his life, are addressed in the next portion of this chapter.

Merton and Zen

It is important in this section to adequately explore Merton's understanding of Zen,[28] his major influences, and those themes he frequently referred to when describing it. Therefore, any statements made here about Zen should be understood as being Merton's understanding or definitions of it, unless another specific person's thought is referenced. This is no attempt to provide any kind of normative or essentialistic definition of Zen, or the "proper" way to understand it. That effort is not necessary for this project, as what is important in this chapter is to explore how Merton understood Zen, and how that influence can be seen in the changing trajectory of his response to the problem of evil.

It is not possible to provide a thorough history of Zen here, but it is important in this overview to provide a brief summary in order to properly contextualize it. Zen, or *Ch'an* as it is known in its native China, grew out of Mahayana Buddhism. One of the original religions of China, Taoism, had prepared the ground for the seed of Zen to grow.[29] Well before Zen developed, Taoism espoused a belief in the superiority of intuitive thought and promoted "an anti-intellectualism that often ridiculed the logic-bound limitations of conventional Chinese life and letters."[30] Some trace the beginning of Zen directly back to the Buddha himself in India. According to legend, the Buddha was once handed a flower and asked to preach about the law. He is said to have taken the flower silently, without a word, wheeling it in his hand. "Then amid the hush his most perceptive follower, Kashyapa, suddenly burst into a smile . . . and thus was born the wordless wisdom of Zen."[31] The understanding of this silent insight was passed down through

28. Some scholars have criticized Merton's understanding and portrayal of Zen for relying too heavily on the work of D. T. Suzuki. For more about this criticism see Keenan, "Limits of Thomas Merton's Understanding of Buddhism"; and for a rebuttal see Dadosky, "Merton's Dialogue with Zen: Pioneering or Passé?"

29. Merton recognized Taoism's influence on Zen. In discussing one of Tao's greatest thinkers, Merton writes, "The true inheritors of the thought and spirit of Chuang Tzu are the Chinese Zen Buddhists of the T'ang period (7th to 10th centuries A.D.)" (Zhuangzi and Merton, *Way of Chuang Tzu*, 15).

30. Hoover, *Zen Experience*, 4.

31. Ibid., 14.

the centuries, independent of the scriptures, finally emerging as the Chinese school of *Chan*, later called Zen by the Japanese."[32]

In the second century CE Indian missionaries began to spread Buddhism in China, and in the fourth century, the Zen of today started to take shape. By the seventh century two kinds of Zen had emerged. First, the northern school affirmed a belief that one gains enlightenment in a step-by-step process. It also posited that there are two different stages of the mind. People are born with a so-called false mind that mistakenly sees the world in a dualistic way. The second stage is the true mind, which overcomes all dualistic distinctions. One can achieve this through a gradual process in which meditation helps transcend dualism. However, in the seventh century the southern school of Zen emerged and challenged that outlook. First, it objected to the notions of a false and true mind. The southern school believed that there is only one reality, and therefore any kind of dualism was false. Its proponents argued that the northern school's distinction between the false and true mind was itself a dualistic notion. In addition, the southern school affirmed that this one reality, or Buddha-mind, is not achieved through any kind of methodical process, as the northern school advocated. Instead one can achieve Buddha-mind all at once, intuitively, and not through any kind of analytical or intellectual process.[33]

In the twelfth century Zen was transmitted to Japan where it quickly gained prominence. Two different schools also emerged there. The Soto school considered enlightenment a gradual process while the Rinzai tradition believed that it can happen suddenly.[34] Thomas Merton's main source for understanding Zen, D. T. Suzuki, was a proponent of the Rinzai tradition. As will be seen, Merton's description of Zen certainly bears out that influence.

Merton's Understanding of Zen

Merton wrote two books during this period that are some of the best sources to identify his understanding of Zen. In *Mystics and Zen Masters*, published in 1967, and *Zen and the Birds of Appetite*, published in 1968, Merton lays out his understanding of Zen and why he finds it to be so appealing. Some Merton critics have asserted that this interest marks a line of

32. Ibid., 6.

33. Ibid., 22.

34. Smith and Novak, *Buddhism*, 208.

demarcation, where Merton had knowingly "wandered from clear Church teaching" and "writes as if his Christianity and his Buddhism had already become enmeshed into a new hybrid religion."[35] However, his journal and other writings during this time clearly show that is not the case. In fact, in supporting his interest in Eastern thought he points to the ecumenical spirit of Vatican II:

> Catholics are now asking themselves, in the words of the Council, how other mystical traditions strive to penetrate "that ultimate mystery which engulfs our being, and whence we take our rise, and whither our journey leads us" (*Declaration on Non-Christian Religions*, n. 1). In doing so, they are guided by the Council's reminder that "the Catholic Church rejects nothing which is true and holy in these religions. She looks with sincere respect upon those ways of conduct and of life, those rules and teachings which, though differing in many particulars from what she holds and sets forth, nevertheless often reflect a ray of that Truth which enlightens all men" (id. 2). Not only must the Catholic scholar respect these other traditions and honestly evaluate the good contained in them, but the Council adds that he must "acknowledge, preserve and promote the spiritual and moral goods found among these men as well as the values in their society and culture" (ibid.).[36]

Remarks Merton made at an interfaith conference in Calcutta approximately a month before he died also clearly express rootedness in his Christian faith, as well as a desire to be enriched through other traditions:

> I speak as a Western monk who is pre-eminently concerned with his own monastic calling and dedication . . . I need not add that I think we have now reached a stage (long overdue) of religious maturity at which it may be possible for someone to remain perfectly faithful to a Christian and Western monastic commitment, and yet to learn in depth from, say, a Buddhist discipline and experience.[37]

---

35. Professor Anthony Clark is uncomfortable with Merton's interest in Eastern thought, and sees those traditions as competitors of Christianity. He expresses concerns that within Buddhism, Zen, and Taoism there is no sense of ultimate good, truth, or God. Clark believes Merton was becoming unmoored from these kinds of ontological Christian truths, and that "his ideas evolve and change often, and his immersion into Eastern religion often appears more like replacement than rapprochement." Clark, "Can You Trust Thomas Merton."

36. Merton, *Mystics and Zen Masters*, viii–ix.

37. Merton, *Asian Journal*, xxiii.

Finally, Merton did not view Zen as another religious system competing with his own Christianity. Instead he states that it "can shine through
this or that system, religious or irreligious, just as light can shine through
glass that is blue, or green, or red, or yellow. If Zen has any preference it
is for glass that is plain, has no color, and is 'just glass.' In other words to
regard Zen merely and exclusively as Zen Buddhism is to falsify it and, no
doubt, to betray the fact that one has no understanding of it whatever."[38]

What then did Merton understand Zen to be? In Zen Merton was attracted to what he believed was a way to directly experience reality—"pure
experience on a metaphysical level"[39]—without any need of external mediation, intellectualization, logical formulations, or even any kind of verbal-
ization.[40] He describes it as a concrete and "lived ontology which explains
itself not as theoretical propositions but in acts that come out of a certain
quality of consciousness and awareness."[41] Zen does not lend itself to logical
analysis. It is not a method of meditation or kind of spirituality. As Merton
describes, it is "a 'way' and an 'experience,' a 'life,' but the way is paradoxi-
cally 'not a way.'"[42] Zen is not by any means a simple withdrawal from the
material world to some kind of interior world of spirit. For Merton, Zen is
in some sense entirely beyond the scope of psychological observation and
metaphysical reflection, and as Merton puts it, "for want of a better term,
we may call it 'purely spiritual.'"[43] Here he is affirming that in Zen one can
gain insights into the true nature of our being through living, and not by
adhering to the strictures of a dogmatic religious belief.

Merton believed that Zen is an awareness potentially already present
in every person, but the individual is not conscious of it. In addition, this
direct or pure experience attained through Zen is not some kind of tran-
scendent experience, where one is imbued with a feeling or realization of
some awareness that comes from outside the individual. As Merton writes,
"Zen is then not Kerygma but realization, not revelation but consciousness,
not news from the Father who sends His Son into this world, but awareness of the ontological ground of our own being here and now, right in the

38. Merton, *Zen and the Birds of Appetite*, 4.

39. Ibid., 43.

40. Ibid., 37.

41. Merton, *Mystics and Zen Masters*, ix–x.

42. Ibid., 12.

43. Ibid., 14.

midst of the world."[44] In this way, Merton believed that Zen does not teach anything; rather it points to a direct or pure awareness of living.[45]

Merton was also attracted to what he understood to be Zen's call to move beyond dualism. He posited that one of the most important things about Zen is its rejection of any kind of dualism. Instead, he wrote that Zen is the ontological awareness of pure being beyond subject and object, and immediate grasp of being in its "suchness" and "thusness."[46] As Merton scholar Bonnie Thurston points out, this line of thought was attractive to him because Zen "provided a corrective to the intellectual dualism engendered by Cartesian thought. (Merton thought we all suffered from trying to travel the spiritual path in a broken Descartes!)"[47] In addition, in his essay "Contemplation and the *Cogito*: Thomas Merton on the Philosophical Roots of Modern Alienation," Ryan Scruggs traces Merton's long held distaste of Cartesian dualism. The following brief example of Merton's own writing about the Cartesian *Cogito* shows his thoughts about this kind of alienation:

> This is the declaration of an alienated being, in exile from his own spiritual depths, compelled to seek some comfort in a proof for his own existence(!) based on the observation that he "thinks." If his thought is necessary as a medium through which he arrives at the concept of his existence, then he is in fact only moving further away from his true being. He is reducing himself to a concept. He is making it impossible for himself to experience, directly and immediately, the mystery of his own being. At the same time, by also

44. Merton, *Zen and the Birds of Appetite*, 47.

45. Ibid., 48.

46. Merton, *Mystics and Zen Masters*, 14. "Suchness" or "thusness" are the English translations of the term, *Tathātā*. This concept, found in the Mahayanan and Zen traditions, refers to an awareness derived from a mundane or everyday act, such as sweeping the floor or looking at a flower. Vietnamese Zen monk Thich Nhat Hanh describes this concept well, writing, "I like to walk alone on country paths, rice plants and wild grasses on both sides, putting each foot down on the earth in mindfulness, knowing that I walk on the wondrous earth. In such moments, existence is a miraculous and mysterious reality. People usually consider walking on water or in thin air a miracle. But I think the real miracle is not to walk either on water or in thin air, but to walk on earth. Every day we are engaged in a miracle which we don't even recognize: a blue sky, white clouds, green leaves, the black, curious eyes of a child—our own two eyes. All is a miracle" (*Miracle of Mindfulness*, 17–18).

47. Thurston, "Light Strikes Home," 23.

reducing God to a concept, he makes it impossible for himself to
have any intuition of the divine reality which is inexpressible.[48]

Because of his problems with Descartes, then, I believe the ground was
already tilled and ready for Zen's idea of nondualism to take seed.

Merton and Suzuki

Merton's main source for understanding Zen was the writings of D. T. Suzuki. He held Suzuki in very high esteem and in fact equated him to Ein-
stein and Gandhi in terms of important figures of that time.[49] In addition,
Merton writes that it was after reading Suzuki that he finally understood
Buddhism and Zen, "whereas before it had been a very mysterious and
confusing jumble of words, images, doctrines, legends, rituals, buildings,
and so forth."[50] In fact, he states that Suzuki's works in English are "without
question the most complete and most authentic presentation of an Asian
tradition and experience by any one man in terms accessible to the West."[51]
Merton goes on to enthuse that Suzuki's work "remains with us as a great
gift, as one of the unique spiritual and intellectual achievements of our
time."[52]

Daisetsu Teitaro Suzuki (1870–1966) was a Japanese author who even
critics[53] recognize was "the single most important figure in the spread of

---

48. Merton, *New Seeds of Contemplation*, 9.

49. Merton, *Zen and the Birds of Appetite*, 59.

50. Ibid., 60.

51. Ibid., 62.

52. Ibid., 64.

53. Suzuki, like Merton, has been criticized for his understanding and presentation
of Zen in the West. For example, Robert Sharf argues that Suzuki's depiction of Zen is
an inaccurate one. In making his case he criticizes Suzuki's formal Zen training, stating
it was "squeezed into weekends and school vacations" (13). In addition, he affirms that
Suzuki's repeated emphasis on the importance of unmediated experience has more in
common with Western philosophical trends of that time, rather than historical Zen (23).
Finally, he argues that Suzuki's claim that Zen is not a distinct religious tradition comes
from a religious tradition that had, a generation before Suzuki, been heavily influenced
by Japanese nationalism. He writes, "Zen, we are told, is immune to 'enlightenment' critiques of religion precisely because it is not a religion in the institutional sense at all . . .
At the same time, the emergent discourse of a reconstructed Zen is predicated upon, and
inexorably enmeshed in, the nativist and imperialist ideology of the late nineteenth- and
early twentieth-century Japan" (5–6). For more see Sharf, "Zen of Japanese Nationalism."

Zen in the West."[54] Suzuki was born in 1870 in the Japanese city of Kanazawa. His father was, like those generations before him, a physician. However, the family struggled financially, due in large part to the loss of their annual rice stipend. At age six Suzuki's family troubles grew much worse when his father died, leaving them in grinding poverty. Tragedy struck again the next year when Suzuki's older brother died. These hardships helped set the trajectory for Suzuki's future life, prompting him as a young man to seek answers to the questions of why he had suffered so much. As Suzuki puts it, "All this I lost, and by the time I was about seventeen or eighteen these misfortunes made me start thinking about my karma. Why should I have these disadvantages at the very start of life?"[55] Suzuki states that his family was of the Zen tradition, and in particular the Rinzai sect. However, describing his religious upbringing, he notes that his father was a Confucian. In addition, in recounting the religiosity of his household as a child, he states, "it would be better to say that there was a religious atmosphere in my family where the spirit of Pure Land Shin Buddhism[56] and Zen was present. My mother did not especially talk about religion."[57]

Around the age of eighteen Suzuki began work as a teacher in a nearby fishing village, teaching math, reading, writing, and some English he had learned.[58] Within the next two years he suffered more loss when his mother died. Shortly after this he went to Tokyo to attend the Imperial University. Once there he became interested in the famous Zen temple Engakuji, in the nearby town of Kamakura. Suzuki began commuting between the university and the temple and eventually took instruction from Zen master Shaku Soen for approximately five years.[59] Suzuki does not describe his time there in glowing terms. In fact, he states that "life in the monastery was exceedingly miserable."[60] Shaku Soen recognized Suzuki's gift for languages and asked him to translate remarks he wrote to deliver at the 1893 World Parliament of Religions that was being held in Chicago. During that event Shaku Soen met a wealthy American business executive who managed a

54. Sharf, ""The Zen of Japanese Nationalism," 12.

55. Suzuki, "Early Memories," 3.

56. Suzuki describes that this kind of Buddhism was prominent in that part of Japan at that time.

57. Suzuki, "Autobiographical Account," 14–15.

58. Gundert, "Sower of Seeds,"136.

59. Ibid. 137.

60. Suzuki, "Autobiographical Account," 19.

publishing house with his son-in-law, Paul Carus. They produced religious and scientific periodicals. Carus made it known he was interested in finding someone to help him with translation work. Shaku Soen introduced Carus to Suzuki, and soon after, Suzuki was heading to the United States. He joined Carus, where he worked for over a decade translating and proofreading for their Open Court imprint and their journal *The Monist*. Suzuki also found time to pursue his own projects, publishing translations of Zen and Buddhist texts.[61] In addition, during this time Suzuki also studied Western philosophy and religion.[62] Suzuki left his position with Carus and the United States in 1908, traveling throughout Europe and Asia. He translated, wrote, and lectured extensively for the next fifty-eight years. In 1966, at the age of ninety-five, he passed away in a Tokyo hospital.

Earlier I mentioned that Merton did not understand Zen as a separate religious belief that competed with his Christianity. This idea came directly from Suzuki:

> Is Zen a religion? It is not a religion in the sense that the term is popularly understood; for Zen has no God to worship, no ceremonial rites to observe, no future abode to which the dead are destined, and, last of all, Zen has no soul whose welfare is to be looked after by somebody else and whose immortality is a matter of intense concern with some people. Zen is free from all these dogmatic and "religious" encumbrances.[63]

In addition, Suzuki describes Zen as transmitting the essence of and spirit of the Buddha, without all the historical Indian doctrinal accretions.[64] The basic idea of Zen for him is to encounter the inner workings of our being, and to do this in the most direct way possible, without resorting to anything external.[65] Further, Suzuki describes Zen in the following four statements: "It is a special transmission outside the Scriptures; there is no dependence upon words and letters; it is the direct pointing to the soul of man; and finally it is seeing into one's nature and the attainment of Buddhahood."[66] In summarizing these points, he emphasizes that Zen points to the nature of one's own being, without any kind of logical analysis

61. Gundert, "Sower of Seeds," 138.

62. Abe, "Problem of Evil in Christianity and Buddhism," 110.

63. Suzuki, *Introduction to Buddhism*, 9.

64. Suzuki, *Essays in Zen Buddhism (First Series)*, 54

65. Suzuki, *Introduction to Buddhism*, 14.

66. Suzuki, *Essays in Zen Buddhism (First Series)*, 19–20.

or intellectualizing.[67] "Zen, therefore, proposes to deal with concrete living facts, and not with dead letters and theories."[68]

An important element of Zen for Suzuki is this kind of sudden and immediate awareness or transcendental wisdom in which dualism is overcome. This is known as *prajna*.[69] This is distinct from the usual kind of knowledge, or *vijnana*, in which we use our intellect and reason, and make dualistic distinctions between subject and object, to conduct the business of our everyday lives.[70] "In *prajna* this differentiation does not take place . . . *Prajna* is the self-knowledge of the whole in contrast to *vijnana*, which busies itself with parts. *Prajna* is an integrating principle while *vijnana* always analyzes."[71] *Prajna* is often compared to a flash of lighting or to a spark from two striking pieces of flint. Here this immediacy, or quickness, does not refer to a chronological passing of time. Rather it points to an immediacy, without any kind of deliberation.[72]

While they have already been touched upon, we must briefly emphasize two elements of Suzuki's thought frequently referenced when Merton describes Zen. Those are its quality of not relying on intellectualization, logical formulas, or schemas; and its call to overcome dualism. Suzuki declared explicitly that Zen does not rely on the intellect for the solution of life's deepest problems.[73] In fact, he asserts that the act of using the intellect or logical reasoning will never be sufficient to thoroughly comprehend the inwardness of a truth or to resolve a problem of deep religious significance.[74] Not only are logic and the intellect ineffectual; one's life as it is lived is often "cut to pieces by recklessly applying the murderous knife of intellectual surgery."[75] Suzuki sees any kind of mediation, deliberation, or logical analysis as an impediment to direct, immediate experience. As he states, "Zen is revealed when we abandon our so-called common-sense

67. Ibid., 20.

68. Suzuki, *Studies in Zen*, 22.

69. Ibid., 55.

70. Ibid., 93–94.

71. Ibid., 85.

72. Ibid., 86–87. This reflects the Taoist influence on Zen, with the elevation of spontaneity over premeditation. For more, see Zhuangzi and Merton, *Way of Chuang Tzu*, 24–28.

73. Suzuki, *Essays in Zen Buddhism (First Series)*, 19.

74. Suzuki, *Mysticism*, 2.

75. Suzuki, *Essays in Zen Buddhism (First Series)*, 26.

or logical attitude and effect a complete about-face, when we plunge right into the working of things as they move on before and behind the scenes. It is only when this experience takes place that we can talk intelligently about Zen-consciousness."[76] The intellect can lead one's mind to a higher level of consciousness by posing a host of questions that are beyond itself. However, those answers, those mysteries are solved only "by living [life], by seeing into its working, by actually experiencing the significance of life, or by tasting the value of living."[77] Suzuki's admonition against overintellectualization is also tied to his affirmation that dualism should be avoided. Dualistic thinking is the product of intellection and is the root of ignorance and thus the ultimate source of suffering in Mahayana and Zen.

Suzuki argues that logical consistency is well and good, but that it is not the end-all, be-all. Dualistic distinctions, the choice between yes and no, present no real problems until one is faced with one of life's "ultimate questions."[78] It is here that one's intellect fails.[79] The following quotation succinctly lays out Suzuki's emphasis on a kind of direct experience that overcomes dualistic distinctions:

> "Ignorance" is another name for logical dualism. White is snow and black is the raven. But these belong to the world and its ignorant way of talking. If we want to get to the very truth of things, we must see them from the point where this world has not yet been created, where the consciousness of this and that has not yet been awakened and where the mind is absorbed in its own identity, that is, in its serenity and emptiness. This is a world of negations but leading to a higher or absolute affirmation—an affirmation in the midst of negations. Snow is not white, the raven is not black, yet each in itself is white or black. This is where our everyday language fails to convey the exact meaning as conceived by Zen.[80]

---

76. Suzuki, *Studies in Zen*, 81.

77. Suzuki, *Mysticism*, 22.

78. Elsewhere Suzuki similarly argues that "an appeal to the analytical understanding is never sufficient to comprehend thoroughly the inwardness of a truth, especially when it is a religious one" (*Essays in Zen Buddhism [First Series]*, 81) In the Mahayana and Zen traditions, language is inherently dualistic. It divides the world into this and that. With that imposed false separation (i.e., ignorance) there are opportunities to grasp, to crave, to hate, and the like. That is the immediate cause of suffering.

79. Suzuki, *Introduction to Zen Buddhism*, 37.

80. Ibid., 21.

Emphasizing these elements of Sukuki's understanding of Zen has been important because these kinds of descriptions often appear when Merton confronts the problem of evil in the last few years of his life.

Merton and the Zen Influence on His Approach to the Problem of Evil

Merton still espoused his purified soul theodicy at the beginning of this final period of his life. However, it is clear that his response to the problem of evil was changing. Two kinds of evidence support my argument that Merton's interest and immersion in Zen played a significant role in changing the way he responded to the problem of evil. The first is a kind of circumstantial or contextual case, examining several aspects of Merton's life during this period that were also influenced by Zen. The second, more direct evidence, comes from examining his statements and writings about the problem of evil during this time and showing how his understanding and description of Zen can be detected in the way he begins to abandon the task of theodicy. I am not arguing that Merton adopted one of the theodicies within the Zen tradition, or that he simply substituted his Christian theodicy for a Zen one. Rather Merton's understanding of Zen, and specifically terms he uses to describe it, are the same ones he uses when confronting the problem of evil—as he increasingly refuses to employ any kind of theodicy as a response to it.

A number of scholars have identified the tremendous influence Zen had on several facets of Merton's life during his last years. Specifically, its influence can be seen in his photography, painting, and poetry during this time. In addition, one can detect its effect in the way Merton held together the contradictory positions of on the one hand being a celibate monk and priest, and on the other hand having a romantic relationship for several months.

Merton and Photography

Paul Pearson, a Merton scholar, and director and archivist of the Thomas Merton Center at Bellarmine University, traces how Merton's interest in Zen influenced his photography in the article "Beyond the Shadow and the Disguise: The Zen Photography of Thomas Merton." Pearson notes that Merton's photography, much like his writing, became a way for him to explore and express his relationship with the world.[81] Merton did not show any real interest in photography until the last years of his life. In a journal entry from September 1964 he describes receiving a camera (a Kodak Instamatic) from a fellow monk to take photos for a picture book the abbot wanted to produce. He took to it quickly, and his excitement about this new pursuit is clear from his reaction to getting his camera back after it had been sent out for repairs: "Camera back. Love affair with camera, so glad to have you back!"[82] Within days Merton makes the first reference to what he called "Zen photography." He writes, "After dinner I was distracted by the dream camera, and instead of seriously reading the Zen anthology I got from the Louisville Library, kept seeing curious things to shoot, especially a mad window in the old tool room of the woodshed. The whole place is full of fantastic and strange subjects—a mine of Zen photography."[83] Merton does not explain what he means by the term "Zen photography." However, in his book *A Hidden Wholeness: The Visual World of Thomas Merton*, author and civil rights activist John Howard Griffin writes that Merton sought to capture photographic images that "might accomplish the slow work of communicating 'a hidden wholeness,' and perhaps reveal some hint of that wordless gentleness that flows out from 'the unseen roots of all created beings.'"[84]

Paul Pearson concludes his essay on the influence of Zen on Merton's photography by stating that in Zen Merton had found a, "'good clean blade' to 'cut right through all the knots;' he also discovered that photography was a tool to assist him in 'going beyond the shadow and the disguise' to the reality that is immediately in front of us, the 'cosmic dance which is always there' and 'beats in our very blood.'"[85] Photography is not the only area in which scholars have identified Zen's influence in Merton's life. His artwork during this period can also reflects this interest.

Merton and Art

Art historian Roger Lipsey recognized the influence of Zen on Merton's drawings during this period and explores this in his article, "Merton,

81. Pearson, "Beyond the Shadow and the Disguise," 184.

82. Merton, *Dancing in the Water of Life*, 149.

83. Ibid., 146.

84. Griffin, *Hidden Wholeness*, 4.

85. Pearson, "Beyond the Shadow and the Disguise," 193.

Suzuki, Zen, Ink: Thomas Merton's Calligraphic Drawings in Context." The son of an artist, Merton had always drawn throughout his life, contributing cartoons to the humor magazine *Jester* at Columbia University and making hundreds of pen-and-ink as well as brush drawings while at Gethsemani.[86] One can see the start of the Zen influence in a journal entry of late 1961, when Merton writes "that the work of art is to be seen—not imagined, worked over intellectually by the viewer. Central is the experience of seeing."[87] This sentiment of "seeing" and not approaching intellectually certainly fits with Merton's understanding and description of Zen. Merton himself described what he understood to be Zen-influenced art:

> The peculiar quality of Chinese and Japanese art that is influenced by Zen is that it is able to suggest what cannot be said, and, by using a bare minimum of form, to awaken us to the formless. Zen painting tells us just enough to alert us to what is not and is nevertheless "right there." Zen calligraphy, by its peculiar suppleness, dynamism, abandon, contempt for "prettiness" and for formal "style," reveals to us something of the freedom which is not transcendent in some abstract and intellectual sense, but which employs a minimum of form without being attached to it, and is therefore free from it."[88]

In late 1963 Merton produced a collection of calligraphic drawings he called shamanic dictation. These drawings were published in the bilingual literary magazine *El Corno Emplumado*. In a letter Merton wrote to its editor, Margaret Randall, his description of how the work should be approached is reminiscent of his understanding of Zen.

> The title I gave them was "Shamanic Dictation" but now, thinking about it, I think it is rather cheap and misleading. You can keep it if you like it, but I think that such calligraphies should really have no literary trimmings at all, including titles . . . These calligraphies (this word is not a title but simply an indication of the species of drawing to which they belong) should really be pure and simple as they are, and they should lay no claim to being anything but themselves. There should be no afterthoughts about them on the part of the artist or spectator. Each time one sees them is the first time. Each stroke is so to speak first and last, all goes in one breath, one

86. Lipsey, "Merton, Suzuki, Zen, Ink," 156–57.

87. Merton, *Turning towards the World*, 180.

88. Merton, *Zen and the Birds of Appetite*, 6.

brushful of ink, and the result is a statement of itself that is "right" insofar as it says nothing "about" anything else under the sun.[89]

Lipsey also recognizes the Zen influence here, and in other works created during this time, stating that Merton's stance against intellectualization or interpretation is "almost certainly" grounded in concepts he encountered in Zen. Finally, Merton gave two collections of his calligraphic drawings the titles of Morning Zen and Midnight Zen; these were exhibited at Catherine Spalding College, now Spalding University, in Louisville, Kentucky, in late 1964. This exhibit went on to be shown in different parts of the country for the next three years.[90] It is clear that Merton believed the art he created during this period was influenced by Zen.

Merton and Poetry

As the first chapter discussed, although Merton played many roles, the role of poet remained important to him through most of his adult life. He composed poems over decades and *The Collected Poems of Thomas Merton*, posthumously published in 1977, contains several hundred works written between 1940 and 1968. In her article "The Light Strikes Home: Notes on the Zen Influence in Merton's Poetry," Merton scholar Bonnie Thurston explores this influence in his later poetry. She quotes from Merton's work *Zen and the Birds of Appetite* to capture a concise definition of what he meant by Zen, distilling it down to be "the quest for direct and pure experience on a metaphysical level, liberated from verbal formulas and linguistic preconceptions,"[91] and "the ontological awareness of pure being beyond subject and object, an immediate grasp of being in its 'suchness' and 'thusness.'"[92] Thurston argues that these themes can be identified in the poetry Merton wrote during his last years; they can be noted both thematically and literarily or technically.[93] While Thurston's detailed article examines many of these facets, I briefly reference two here. First, acknowledging Merton's indebtedness to Suzuki as his primary source of understanding Zen, Thurston points to several of Merton's poems that exhibit Suzuki's six

89. Merton, *Courage for Truth*, 216–17.

90. Lipsey, *Angelic Mistakes*, 29.

91. Merton, *Zen and the Birds of Appetite*, 44.

92. Ibid., 14.

93. Thurston, "Light Strikes Home," 200–201.

verbal methods for attaining an "idea of absolute oneness." Those are paradox, going beyond opposites, contradiction, affirmation, repetition and exclamation.[94] In addition, Thurston contends that in some of Merton's longer poems, such as "Geography of Lograire," he was working on at the time of his death, pushing the limits of language. She asserts that the impetus for this pushing "was at least in part Merton's appropriation of Buddhism, especially Zen."[95] She also points to other works, such as "Cables to the Ace" that contain these themes. Thurston concludes her article arguing that "in Merton's later poetry his study of Zen manifests itself in a preference for the concrete, for the truth found in experience rather than abstraction or speculative thinking."[96]

The work of Pearson, Lipsey, and Thurston illustrate many of the ways Merton's life was influenced by his understanding of Zen. One more example is left to be examined: the way that Merton employed aspects of Zen, as he understood it, to make sense of and justify a romantic relationship he had while living as a priest and monk.

Merton and His Affair

Merton's romantic relationship was briefly discussed in chapter 1. On March 23, 1966, he entered St. Joseph's Infirmary, in nearby Louisville, Kentucky, to have surgery on his cervical spine. While recuperating he met a young student nurse, and the two soon developed a friendship. What started with letters and calls soon led to visits and romantic encounters. Merton did not ever seriously consider abandoning his vocation as a priest to be with M, and the physical component of their relationship concerned him. In his journal Merton describes one episode from late May 1966, "We got ourselves quite aroused sexually last Thursday . . . there is no question that this cannot become a sexual affair, it would be disastrous for us both. It simply must not happen. Also she is too curious about all that—and too passionate for me (her body to tell the truth was wonderful the other day, ready for the most magnificent love)."[97] In addition, there was an encounter that summer that progressed further than Merton had intended. He had arranged to meet M alone at his psychiatrist's office and brought a bottle

94. Ibid., 208.
95. Ibid., 200.
96. Ibid., 211.
97. Merton, *Learning to Love*, 69–70.

of champagne. Merton had used his doctor's office, when it was not in use, during past visits to Louisville to read and write between appointments.[98] While he does not describe the specifics of this encounter, Merton biographer Michael Mott writes that Merton "believed he was in trouble with his vow."[99] As Merton notes in his journal, "I keep remembering her body, her nakedness, the day at Wygal's, and it haunts me."[100] This issue is important to address because this romantic relationship was clearly in contradiction with Merton's professed life as a monk and priest. Interestingly, Merton can be seen using descriptions and concepts of Zen to justify it to himself.

Merton frequently describes Zen as being formless and without logical formulas or schemas. Such language occurs as he tries to justify the relationship to himself. He writes in his journals: "Awoke with the deep realization that my response to love to M was right. It might have nothing to do with the rulebooks or with any other systems, it might be open to all kinds of delusions and air, but in fact so far by and large I have been acting right."[101]

In this next journal passage Merton writes that their relationship could not be comprehended using the intellect: "When we began, we knew it could not be understood. As we went along we wanted it to be understandable, and it never was. There is nothing understandable in love: just joy and sorrow and if you are lucky, more joy."[102] As has been discussed, this same quality applies to Merton's understanding of Zen.

I have described the quality of nondualism that enthralled Merton. He tried to reconcile his relationship with M and his monastic life by appealing to this same nondualism. Several entries in his journal show this: "I thought of God's love for her and mine. I can see absolutely no reason why my love for her and for Christ should necessarily be separated and opposed . . . but if I love her purely and unselfishly—as I surely do here in solitude—then my love for her is part of my love for him, part of the offering of myself to God."[103]

This notion of nondualism is also clearly expressed in the following passage: "What really is God's will for me? To live where I am living—to

98. Mott, *Seven Mountains*, 444.

99. Ibid., 444.

100. Merton, *Learning to Love*, 94.

101. Ibid., 45.

102. Ibid., 309.

103. Ibid., 99.

remain here—to be faithful to the grace of solitude—yet also a certain fidelity to my deep affections for M—though this seems to involve a pure contradiction. And yet it does not per se. Only in a selfish exploitation would it become wrong."[104]

This next journal entry is a particularly good example of how nondualism reconciled his two kinds of life. "I no longer know what these things mean, or what their opposites might mean. I am not passing from this to something that stands against it. I am not going anywhere. I exist because I have the habit of existing."[105]

In yet another entry one can see how the nondualism and nonanalytical elements of Zen influenced Merton as he tried to reconcile his life as a monk and his relationship with M. This is seen when he writes:

> What is my life? My solitude? The determination to be lucid and quiet and to wait, and to nourish the unspeakable hope of deep love which is beyond analysis and is so far down it has no voice left. Down there we are one voice: the voice of your womanness blends with the man I am, and we are one being, completing each other, though we no longer can express it by taking each other in our arms.[106]

Finally, in the following passage Merton explicitly invokes Zen to reconcile his monastic life with his relationship.

> I was thinking of what some old Zen joker said about "until you know the mind is no mind you do not understand it" and of course he is right: all the worried thoughts I have had today are not "my mind" and the thinking that goes on when I am like that is not "my mind." Whatever it is, it is not I. And then I realized how free one can really be. All these worries and anxieties had nothing to do with love either . . . love is quite free and unconditional. It loves without seeking to explain itself even to itself. It does not, in other words, look for conditions under which it is reasonable to love, or right to love, it simply loves. And that is how I really love M. I love her unconditionally, straight, and always will. Because I will not be looking for conditions that will change it. True, externally we are hindered, but that does nothing to the essence of a love which is unconditional, for I do not say I will stop loving when I cannot

104. Ibid., 120.
105. Ibid., 302–3.
106. Ibid., 306.

see her or hold her close to me. I simply love. And all these worries about it are silly.[107]

Section Summary

A number of scholars have explored how Merton's interest in Zen can be seen in a variety of ways in the last years of his life. While still squarely Christian, Merton was very interested in, and influenced by, his understanding of Zen, and D. T. Suzuki was his primary source. This influence can be seen in the art, poetry, and photography that he produced during this period. In addition, I have endeavored to show how he also employed ideas of Zen to overcome the seeming contradiction between his life as a priest and monk with the romantic affair he had in the summer of 1966.[108] All of this is meant to support my argument that this same influence can be seen as contributing to the change in the way Merton addressed the problem of evil during this period. This argument does not just rest on this contextual evidence alone. In addition, I assert that this influence can also be seen by examining how Merton directly addresses the problem of evil in the last years of his life. That is the focus of the following section.

Merton's Changing Response to the Problem of Evil: The Abandonment of the Task of Theodicy

Camus Revisited

Having described Merton's understanding of Zen and aspects of it that appealed to him, we can now examine the rest of his work during this last part of his life, to see the ways his understanding of Zen influenced his thoughts about God, evil, and suffering. In fact, it is possible to detect this in examining the rest of Merton's writings about Camus. I have already addressed some of Merton's comments about *The Plague*, and I resume that analysis now. Merton comments on an exchange between two of the characters, Dr. Rieux, the atheistic doctor, and Fr. Paneloux, a Jesuit priest who sees the plague as God's retribution for the community's sinful ways. In the part of

107. Ibid., 335.

108. Other scholars have also gestured towards this same conclusion. For more see Fox, *Way to God*, 190; and Habito, "Hearing the Cries of the World," 113.

the story before us now, the doctor and priest have just witnessed the painful death of a child, and Merton describes the scene, and more importantly, addresses the problem of evil in a new way.

> Paneloux no longer has any glib explanation, but only suggests that we must love what we cannot understand. Rieux replies, "I have a different conception of love. And I shall refuse to the bitter end this scheme of things in which children are tortured." This is a caricature of the theology of evil. Does Christianity demand that one "Love a system, an explanation, a scheme of things" which for its coherence demands that people be tortured? Is that what the Gospel and the Cross mean? To some Christians, unfortunately, yes. And it is they that present Camus with an absurdity against which he must revolt.[109]

This brief passage is important for two reasons. First, it represents a marked departure from what had been Merton's consistent response to the problem of evil: i.e., that God allows and sometimes causes suffering to produce a good, the purification of the human soul. That had been his answer for decades. Second, the purified soul theodicy was anchored in a theological framework to help explain why people suffered. This analytical approach was best exemplified when Merton spoke to the group of monks after the assassination of President Kennedy. He explained, in part, that evil acts such as that one are "part of a whole complex of causes and effects, all of which God willed."[110] However, in these comments on *The Plague* Merton's usual response to evil and suffering is nowhere to be found. This is the first of several instances when Merton does not simply move from one particular theodicy to another. Rather, increasingly during these last few years of his life, he refuses to engage in the task of theodicy altogether.

In the same essay Merton states that Camus frames the problem of evil as "an aesthetic one that cannot really be solved by logic or metaphysics, a question of structure that is unsatisfactory because it lacks harmony and unity—it is in fact to him aesthetically and morally absurd."[111] Merton's response again reveals thoughts and vocabulary that he used to express his understanding of Zen: "What is crucially important in our world is not evil as an abstract scenario but evil as a existential fact. It is here that Camus

---

109. Merton, "Camus and the Church," 263.

110. Merton, *President's Death*.

111. Merton, "Camus and the Church," 266.

speaks most clearly to the church."[112] Merton rejects formulaic responses, logical mediation, or an "abstract scenario" that attempts to understand how evil and suffering fit into God's plan.

In addition to his writings about Camus, other works during this period suggest that Merton's response to the problem of evil seems to be influenced by his understanding of Zen. In addressing the issue as presented in the work of Julian of Norwich, Merton's treatment of the subject is again different from his long held position. That is clear when he writes:

> there exists no satisfactory intellectual solution. It is, even in spite of revelation, a problem that has not yet been fully solved and cannot be solved until the end of time when Christ Himself will make known something that has never been revealed before: the secret which He alone knows, and which it is not given us to know, which not even the blessed in heaven have yet seen, because it is not necessary for our salvation.[113]

Here again, Merton's response echoes what he believed was the Zen call not to rely on the intellect in order to gain true insight. D. T. Suzuki repeatedly writes that the intellect cannot provide answers to such difficult problems "But when it comes to the question of life itself we cannot wait for the ultimate solution to be offered by the intellect, even if it could do so."[114]

Zen Influence on Merton's Theodicy as Seen in Correspondence

Elements of this Zen influence on Merton's attitude about the problem of evil can also be found in some of his correspondence during this time. First, in the spring of 1967, Merton responded to a letter from a Jeanette Yakel, of Green Island, New York, who had written him asking why God permits cruelty to animals. She wrote that it seems to be "so unjust and needless."[115] Once again, Merton's response contains a number of ideas worth unpacking. He begins by stating that "any question about unjust and useless suffering is difficult to answer, and I must admit that I do not have ready answers to such questions at hand."[116] This stands in stark contrast to the "ready an-

112. Ibid., 266.

113. Merton, *Mystics and Zen Masters*, 144.

114. Suzuki, *Essays in Zen Buddhism (First Series)*, 18.

115. Merton, *Road to Joy*, 347.

116. Ibid.

swer" that he had used for the last two decades. In this first line of Merton's response he is again backing away from his long espoused purified soul theodicy. In fact, in his next sentence he seems to directly contradict it: "In the end, I believe the trouble comes from some imperfect way in which we imagine God 'willing' or 'permitting' these things, as if He were somehow a human being and outside of everything. Who knows?"[117] This position is clearly different from the ones that Merton had taken over the previous two decades, repeatedly stating that God allows and sometimes causes suffering. Merton's letter continues:

> If human suffering has value, it is only from the fact that Christ, God Himself, suffers it in us and with us. Who is to say that He does not in some way Himself suffer in the animals what they suffer? That is a possible answer. God cannot simply look on "objectively" while His creatures suffer. To imagine Him doing so is to imagine something quite other than God. I do not say that the sufferings of animals have a supernatural meritorious value and all that: but perhaps they do have some special meaning that is not clear to us. In any case, from the natural scientific point of view it can be said that the sufferings of animals are radically different from ours in so far as they do not have the same kind of highly developed imagination we have: they do not add the mental suffering that we add on to physical suffering.[118]

In this section of the letter Merton returns to elements of cruciform theodicy, pointing out that Christ suffers with us and provides hope of redemption at the time of the eschaton. Interestingly, as if this thematic return to his earlier position reminded him of his long held belief that suffering can result in some kind of good here and now, Merton next writes, "Note also that the physical organism may benefit in some way by fighting back against pain. We often experience that in ourselves. These are just suggestions. In any case, human beings who wantonly cause animals to suffer are certainly very much to blame."[119] This letter is fascinating: it clearly shows Merton's changing response to the problem of evil, which is his increasing refusal to do the work of theodicy. In addition his declaration that he does not have any kind of logical, formulaic response, or "ready answers" is

117. Ibid.
118. Ibid.
119. Ibid.

certainly reminiscent of his repeated description of Zen not relying on the intellect to gain insights.

A second letter written during this time also illustrates this Zen influence. On April 5, 1968, the day after Martin Luther King Jr.'s assassination, Merton wrote to Dr. King's widow, Coretta Scott King. His only comment to her pertaining to the why of the tragedy is, "Some events are too big and terrible to talk about."[120] This statement is starkly different from ones in letters to the Kennedy family just five years earlier, when Merton wrote that God would bring some good out of the president's assassination. Writing about the JFK assassination, Merton had stated that "we must see it as a warning once again to the whole country,"[121] and that "I think it is beginning to be clear that God allowed this that He might bring great good out of it."[122] D. T. Suzuki wrote frequently about Zen's attitude toward the use of intellect and specifically toward the use of language and "words" to help one gain deep insights. As Suzuki put it, "The highest and most fundamental experiences are best communicated without words; in the face of such experiences we become speechless and stand almost aghast."[123] Admittedly Merton's one sentence, "Some events are too big and terrible to talk about," is too fragmentary an example from which to draw any large conclusions. However, placed in context, and with other writings about the problem of evil during this time, I do believe it shows how Zen, or at least concepts and vocabulary used by Suzuki, were influencing Merton's response to the problem of evil.

THE DEATH OF AUNT KIT

In April of 1968 Merton received news of the death of Agnes Gertrude Stonehewer Merton, or Aunt Kit.[124] She died April 10, 1968, drowned when the New Zealand interisland ferry Wahine sank in Wellington Harbor. At

120. Merton, *Hidden Ground of Love*, 451.

121. Ibid., 447.

122. Ibid., 450.

123. Suzuki, *Studies in Zen*, 65.

124. "Kit" Merton (1889–1968). One of Merton's paternal aunts, she was the New Zealand relative whom Merton knew best in his later years. She had been a schoolteacher in New Zealand, in Australia, and, for a year, in England. She never married, making her home in Christchurch with her mother and sister, Beatrice Katharine Merton ["Aunt Ka"]. She retired from the Christchurch Girls' High School in 1947. In November 1961 she surprised Merton by visiting him at Gethsemani. Merton, *Road to Joy*, 59.

this stage of his life Merton considered her to be one of his closest relatives, and the news was understandably difficult to hear.[125] Merton's writings about this loss provide more insights about his idea of God's role in suffering, and again the influence of Zen can be detected. First, in a letter to his Aunt Ka[126] he wrote:

> I was terribly shocked and saddened, and I know you must all be very distressed. Such things are so hard to grasp and understand. One remains completely stunned by them for a long time, especially since the whole thing took on the shape of a national tragedy with homes wrecked by the storm, communications disrupted and all the rest. One feels so helpless at the finality of such things.[127]

Much like his letter to Coretta Scott King written that year, this letter makes no attempt to relate events to God's will, or explain them in terms of being a part of a large divine schema. Instead Merton simply refuses to engage in the task of theodicy, stating that "such things are so hard to grasp and understand."

Merton also reflected on his aunt's death in his journal, and that entry is certainly worth examination.

> What can be said about such things? Nothing will do. Absurdity won't. An awful sense that somehow it had to be this way because it was, and no one can say why, really. And yet "what did she ever do to deserve it?" Such a question does not make sense, and the God I believe in is not one who can be "blamed," for it is he who suffers this incomprehensibility in me more than I do myself. But there is a stark absence of all relatedness between the quiet, gentle, unselfish courage of Aunt Kit's life and this dreadful, violent death. What have these waves and currents to do with her?[128]

This passage is fascinating because it certainly shows how his thoughts about evil and suffering had developed and were changing in this last period of his life. For example, the more recent Zen influence seems apparent

---

125. In a letter he wrote after her death he says, "She was probably the closest to me among my surviving family, the only one with whom I regularly corresponded, so it is a real loss" (Merton, *Road to Joy*, 85).

126. Beatrice Katharine Merton (1891–1972) was Merton's other paternal aunt. She was a nurse in Christchurch, New Zealand. She visited him once, in 1922, when he was living in the United States (Merton, *Road to Joy*, 64).

127. Merton, *Road to Joy*, 84.

128. Merton, *Other Side of the Mountain*, 85.

in his introductory statement: "What can be said about such things? Nothing will do," reflects Zen's notion that words are insufficient to arrive at deep insights. In addition, Merton is definitely backing away from directly implicating God in this event. Once again, this stands in stark contrast to earlier statements, such as "God wants us to suffer because perfection is attained only through suffering. Then too, by suffering we undergo punishment which is rightly meted out."[129] Apparent from this journal entry is Merton's real reluctance to rely on his purified soul theodicy.

Contemplating Scripture

Merton also provides relevant insights into his understanding of suffering in an essay he wrote in 1967. In particular, Suzuki's influence on his changing stance towards the problem of evil can be seen in it. In "Opening the Bible," an essay he wrote to be used as an introduction to a Time-Life edition of the Bible, Merton affirms that some positive outcome can arise from suffering.

> Suffering is a symptom of disorder, and if we can understand its message, we can learn how to become once again unified and reconciled with ourselves and with God. The problem of suffering resides in our mistaken determination to get rid of all suffering while resolutely maintaining the division and protecting the split off ego-self which is the focus of suffering."[130]

A few key thoughts must be examined from this short quote. First, Merton's assertion that some good can come from evil not only corresponds to his purified soul theodicy but is also reminiscent of Suzuki's thought that "the more you suffer the deeper grows your character, and with the deepening of your character you read the more penetratingly into the secrets of life . . . Unless you eat your bread in sorrow, you cannot taste of real life."[131]

In addition, Merton's admonition that the problem of suffering resides in trying to eliminate it certainly echoes Suzuki's statement that "the value of human life lies in the fact of suffering, for where there is no suffering, no consciousness of karmic bondage, there will be no power of attaining spiritual experience and thereby reaching the field of non-distinction. Unless

---

129. Merton, *Life of Vows,* 54.

130. Merton, *Opening the Bible,* 77.

131. Suzuki, *Essays in Zen Buddhism (First Series),* 16.

we agree to suffer we cannot be free from suffering."[132] We know Merton was familiar with, and impressed by, this quotation because Merton himself referred to it in his book *Zen and the Birds of Appetite*.[133]

Finally, Merton locates the "focus of suffering" in the dualism of "maintaining the division and protecting the split off ego-self." This is certainly reminiscent of Suzuki's repeated call to overcome dualism.

The Alaskan Conference

Finally, aspects of Suzuki's influence are perhaps best seen in Merton's comments in a lecture given while in Alaska in September 1968. He had stopped there to give a series of lectures and conference presentations before leaving for his much-anticipated trip to Asia. In the following remarks Merton not only addresses the book of Job and the problem of evil, but does so in a way that reflects Suzuki's influence on his current response to the problem of evil.

> Any theology in which we pretend to justify God by reason is bound to be bad theology. You cannot do it. It is the theology of Job's friends. The Book of Job tells us a great deal about prayer. It says that here is a man who undergoes great evil and here are four people who come along and explain the evil logically and they tell Job why he is wrong and why he has to suffer. We talk about the patience of Job, but Job is not patient at all. In fact, he is mad at God and he is arguing with God and he is protesting against God and saying you are not right, you are wrong, you shouldn't be doing this to me. And what happens at the end of it is that God comes along and says Job is right.[134]

Here Merton seems influenced by Suzuki—especially in the admonition that the use of any kind of logical formula, or "reason," to make sense of this and to justify evil in light of God's divine will is futile. This Zen attitude is also present as he continues:

> This is real theology, because it is not logical. And the real theological message of this is not that God hits people over the head to show that He is there but that our relations with God are person-to-person relationships, and that we don't deal with God according to

132. Ibid., 13

133. Merton, *Zen and the Birds of Appetite*, 94.

134. Merton, *Thomas Merton in Alaska*, 117–18.

some system. You don't look up in a book, asking yourself, "How do I talk to God about this?" Something evil has happened in your life. So you look in the book, and the book says, "God permits evil for your good," and you say, "Oh well, all right." There is nothing wrong with this, but the Bible says that if you really talk with God and say what is in your heart you are doing right. You speak to God as a child to a father and you go to Him and tell Him what you want Him to know and then He tells you what He wants you to know, and this puts it on a completely person-to-person basis. You don't get to God through a system. You speak from your heart. That is the basic idea, and that is what the Book of Job is saying.

Once again this recommendation that one should not use a system or logic in an attempt to understand evil and suffering certainly matches Merton's understanding of Zen's approach to gaining insights into the nature of our being and into wisdom. Finally, Suzuki's emphasis that Zen contains an anti-systematized ethos is clearly seen in these last remarks:

> You realize that prayer takes us beyond the law . . . In other words, if there are no laws, then there is no law of prayer, there are no systems. Systems are fine up to a point, but all they are for is to help you get to the point where there is no more system, where you deal with God absolutely in your freedom and His freedom.[135]

The comments made at this conference are important for several reasons. First, they were delivered in the last three months of Merton's life while he was on his way to Asia. His interest and immersion in Zen was at its highest point. In addition, he returns to the subject of evil and suffering, only now there are few hints of his long espoused purified soul theodicy. These remarks are telling in that they do not attempt to show that suffering is in any way a part of God's will, or as he put it to his novices after the JFK assassination, "part of a large complex of causes and effects all of which God wills."[136] Instead, Merton moves away from the work of theodicy. That is, he abandons any effort to provide an explanation or understanding of how an all-loving and all-powerful God could allow evil and suffering. Now, when confronting the problem of evil, he directly states that one cannot use logic or systems—a theodicy—to arrive at any satisfactory answers.

135. Ibid., 119.
136. Merton, *President's Death*.

Summary

This third and last period of Merton's life as a writer, from 1964 through 1968, starts with him continuing to espouse his purified soul theodicy in a variety of writings. In addition, he becomes captivated by the work of Albert Camus, whose work *The Plague* dealt with a stereotypical Christian response to the problem of evil. In commenting on this point, Merton rejects belief in a God who metes out harsh punishment with no concern for the suffering of humanity. Merton uses the essays on Camus to explore his idea that in its "Death of God" age humanity is no longer oriented toward God, and therefore grotesque evils such as the Holocaust, as well as other atrocities, are the inevitable outcomes in a world pointed toward humanity rather than God.

Merton's writings particularly about evil and suffering, and how they fit into God's will, take a decidedly different turn. Elements of his long held purified soul theodicy can still be found, largely in the early part of this period. However, given the tantalizingly few references to the problem of evil during this time, enough emerge to clearly show how Merton's approach changes. This change involves not simply the substitution of one theodicy for another. Instead, Merton abandons the task of theodicy altogether. During this period he increasingly responds to the issue of suffering, and specifically the problem of evil, by stating that the intellect, logic, theories or schemas for how suffering fits into the divine plan, fail to provide satisfactory answers. As we have seen, this response departs significantly from Merton's long held purified soul theodicy. What could have caused such a change?

I have argued that interest and immersion in Zen during this period, as understood through the writings of D. T. Suzuki, influenced Merton's changing response to the problem of evil. To support that argument, I made a contextual case, showing how other scholars have already pointed to areas of Merton's life influenced by Zen. Specifically, others have argued that during this same period when Merton was moving away from his long espoused theodicy, Zen's influence can be detected on his art, poetry, and photography. In itself this contextual evidence is compelling for explaining why his views changed. However, Merton's own writing and speaking about the problem of evil during this time must also be carefully considered. A thorough review of these primary sources indicates that they support my contention that Zen, as understood through Suzuki's writings, contributed to Merton's changing position on suffering and the problem of evil.

Although Merton does not write extensively about these topics during his final years, instances that are present have a common theme. That is, now when confronting this issue, Merton more often than not states that one cannot use a theodicy (logic or systems) to arrive at any satisfactory answers, and his appreciation of Zen is the best explanation of this new position. The very language that he uses to make his case is the same language he also employs to explain his and Suzuki's understanding of Zen aspects. For example, Merton's comment that "there exists no satisfactory intellectual solution" to the problem of evil[137] clearly echoes Suzuki's writing that life's ultimate questions "cannot be solved on the plane of intellection. The intellect raises the question, but fails to give a satisfactory solution."[138] During Merton's final years he also concedes that words often fall short in confronting the problem of evil. Here again, his views align with statements that Suzuki made: for example, "the highest and most fundamental experiences are best communicated without words; in the face of such experiences we become speechless and stand almost aghast."[139] Finally, Merton declares that "systems are fine up to a point, but all they are for is to help you get to the point where there is no more system, where you deal with God absolutely in your freedom and His freedom."[140] This statement clearly echoes Suzuki's claim that "an appeal to the analytical understanding is never sufficient to comprehend thoroughly the inwardness of a truth, especially when it is a religious one."[141]

Again I define the boundaries of my argument: I do not contend that Merton's immersion in Zen was conclusively or even the sole factor that caused him to abandon the task of theodicy in the last years of his life. There could be other unexpressed reasons. However, it is a demonstrable fact that Merton's response to the problem of evil did indeed change during his last years. In addition, his interest in Zen had reached its zenith during this time, and strong evidence supports that Zen influenced several aspects of Merton's life. Further, the language Merton uses to advocate a move away from any kind of theodicy features some of the same concepts and vocabulary with which he and Suzuki describe Zen. Finally, I do not argue that Merton's deep grasp of Zen concepts (e.g., its answer to the problem of evil

137. Merton, *Mystics and Zen Masters,* 144.
138. Suzuki, *Mysticism,* 22.
139. Suzuki, *Studies in Zen,* 65.
140. Merton, *Thomas Merton in Alaska,* 119.
141. Suzuki, *Essays in Zen Buddhism (First Series),* 81.

as overcoming dualism, or Zen's emphasis on interdependence between good and evil) led to his adopting them. The evidence does not prove such a conclusion. Rather, what seems clear is that Merton was influenced by Suzuki's insistent argument that the intellect is ultimately lacking in providing the needed insights into life's ultimate questions, especially religious ones. That then increasingly became Merton's response to the problem of evil in the last years of his life.

With the close of this chapter it is now possible, in the following brief concluding chapter, to pull together ideas from all four chapters and draw some overall conclusions.

Conclusion

Thomas Merton was a remarkable figure. His writing and work had a profound effect on a diverse group of people—those interested in the contemplative life, mysticism, and a possible Christian response to the social ills of the day. Many Christians and non-Christians alike continue to be drawn to his unceasing effort to be closer to God. In addition, Merton's interest in and dialogue with other faiths, especially Zen Buddhism and Buddhism in general, make him a useful model for interfaith dialogue. Even though he was largely removed from the world, in the last part of his life he was greatly interested in a host of social and global issues. Merton clearly expressed his concerns about the continued stockpiling of nuclear weapons by the United States, as well as its escalation in the Vietnam War. He also spoke out about race relations and the alienating tendency inherent in technology. Finally, many are interested in this fascinating human figure, not in spite of his roiling contradictions, but because of them. For all of these reasons, it is likely that Merton will continue to be a figure to study for many years to come.

Merton wrote over sixty books over a twenty-five-year period, and new collections of previously unpublished writings are still being published, almost fifty years after his death. In addition, hundreds of hours of audio recordings of lectures and other unpublished materials have been collected at the Thomas Merton Center at Bellarmine University. With so much material, it is imperative that one examine the entire body of work, or at least as much of it as possible, in order to properly evaluate what Merton truly believed about a particular subject. As one scholar and acquaintance of Merton observed, this can at times be a daunting task, "One difficulty in grasping Merton is that he wrote so voluminously and covered so many topics in both depth and breadth that one can get a little lost trying to grasp the entirety of his thought."[1] As I mentioned earlier, Merton recognized the need for one to take a wide view of his work. As he put it, "My ideas are always changing, always moving around one center, always seeing the center from somewhere else. I will always be accused of inconsistencies—and will no longer be there to hear the accusation."[2]

My goal in this book has been to take this wide view of Merton's entire work to determine his understanding of God's role in human suffering. Merton does, clearly and consistently, espouse a belief that God allows and in some cases causes suffering for particular ends, and specifically, for the purification of the human soul. Thus, I have named his approach a purified soul theodicy. One can find this belief within Merton's thought, as he repeatedly expressed it in a number of books, pieces of correspondence, and remarks he made to fellow religious over twenty-five years of his adult life. Traces of this belief are present in his writing as early as 1940, and it continued to be his default response to the problem of evil for almost the rest of his life.

Merton's purified soul theodicy was not unique in affirming that some good can be produced as a result of suffering. Most theodicies affirm that notion either explicitly or implicitly. For example, as we saw in chapter 2, free will and soul-making theodicies both find some benefit from suffering. However, free will theodicy is careful to assert that moral evil is created by humanity itself. Soul-making theodicy posits that moral evil is the predictable result of humanity still succumbing to some of its baser animalistic instincts that resulted from humanity being created at an epistemic distance from God. While free will and soul-making theodicies differ in many areas, one important point of agreement is that God does not directly cause the day-to-day suffering of human beings. While one may question and criticize a God who chose to create a world where such suffering occurs, God is not directly to be blamed for it. However, what does seem different about Merton's purified soul theodicy, compared to the other prominent Christian responses to the problem of evil, is his unflinching affirmation that at times God actively causes human suffering in order to bring about a good. Time and again he affirmed that belief, and unequivocally stated, for example, that "God wants us to suffer because perfection is attained only

1. Fox, *Way to God*, 47.
2. Merton, *Dancing in the Water of Life*, 67.

through suffering."[3] It is important to remember that Merton also stressed that God joins with us when we suffer.

It is not hard to envision that some may find this approach to the problem of evil to be disquieting. However, it should be noted that in many instances in our everyday life suffering is a known or possible result in order to bring about a good. Painful surgery to mend a broken limb and side effects from medicines used to cure illness are two such examples. In addition, parents are far too familiar with this reality. When I took my ill daughter to the doctor for a shot, I actively caused her suffering. Similarly, when I insisted she remain a part of a sports or extracurricular group that she wanted to quit, in order to teach the lesson of honoring commitments and persevering through adversity, I knew suffering was likely. The intent in both cases was to bring about particular good outcomes. Every theodicy has aspects that one may find problematic or unappealing. The task of theodicy is not to offer a conclusive answer to the problem of evil but rather guide exploration of the subject. In addition, I have not evaluated in these pages the appeal of any particular theodicy, including Merton's. Finally, I have made the case that Merton's purified soul theodicy, though consistently affirmed for decades, was not his final stance towards the problem of evil.

In the last years of his life Merton began abandoning the task of theodicy altogether. During this period, he does address the problem of evil several times in writings and remarks made at a conference, but gone is his long held response to the problem of evil. Now, for example, when confronted with such tragedies as the Martin Luther King Jr. assassination or the sudden death of his own family member, Merton can find no reason for such losses. In fact, during the last years of his life he refuses to engage in the task of theodicy. That is, Merton does not attempt to offer explanations, based on logic or any kind of intellectualization, as to how an all-loving and all-powerful God could allow evil and suffering. What can explain this change? I have argued that Merton's interest and immersion in Zen through the writings of D. T. Suzuki strongly contributed to this changing response to the problem of evil. Merton did not simply adopt one of the responses to the problem of evil found in Zen. Rather, he employed concepts and vocabulary found in Zen to express his new approach. Merton's new approach included an admonition against using logic, intellectualization, or even words to confront the problem of evil. This new attitude clearly echoes Suzuki's statement, for example, that "an appeal to the analytical

3. Merton, *Life of Vows*, 54.

understanding is never sufficient to comprehend thoroughly the inward-ness of a truth, especially when it is a religious one."[4] I have tried to offer a thorough review of the evidence—both the work of other scholars demon-strating the impact Zen had on Merton's art, photography, and poetry, as well as a careful review of his own writings during this time—to support my contention that Zen, as understood through Suzuki, contributed to Merton's changing approach to the problem of evil.

Finally, it is vital to point out that Merton never called for acquiescence in the face of evil in this world. He did not believe that one should passively accept suffering or evil. Rather, both are to be opposed. As Merton wrote, "If evil comes into our life, it is in order that we may grow and give glory to God by cooperating with him in resisting it."[5] In the last decade of his life, while seeking more seclusion from the world, he was the most immersed in its problems. Merton wrote extensively about the need for humanity to defeat racism, avoid wars and nuclear proliferation, and work for peace. His call to oppose evil was not vague, or divorced from the practical realities of the day. At times Merton provided concrete plans to combat social ills. For example, in writing about his opposition to the nuclear arms race, he pro-posed that "it seems to me that Christian morality imposes on every single one of us the obligation to protest against it and to work for the creation of an international authority with power and sanctions that will be able to control technology, and divert our amazing virtuosity into the service of man instead of against him."[6] Therefore one should not believe that Merton advocated a surrender to evil at any point in his life. Even though he could find God's hand in allowing and even causing suffering, Merton repeatedly sought ways to conquer the humanly caused evils of alienation and hatred that lead to suffering, in order to usher in Christ's promised kingdom of God here and now.

4. Suzuki, *Essays in Zen Buddhism (First Series)*, 81.

5. Merton, *Love and Living*, 180.

6. Merton, *Peace in a Post-Christian Era*, 105.

Bibliography

Abe, Masao. "The Problem of Evil in Christianity and Buddhism." In *Buddhist-Christian Dialogue: Mutual Renewal and Transformation,* edited by Paul O. Ingram and Frederick J. Streng, 139–54. 1986. Reprint, Eugene, OR: Wipf & Stock, 2007.

Adams, Marilyn M. "Afterword." In *Encountering Evil: Live Options in Theodicy,* edited by Stephen T. Davis, 191–203. Atlanta: John Knox, 1981.

———. "Redemptive Suffering: A Christian Solution to the Problem of Evil." In *The Problem of Evil: Selected Readings,* 169–87. Library of Religious Philosophy 8. Notre Dame, IN: University of Notre Dame Press, 1992.

———. "Horrendous Evils and the Goodness of God." In *Horrendous Evils and the Goodness of God,* 209–21. Ithaca: Cornell University Press, 1999.

Augustine, of Hippo, Saint. *City of God.* Translated by Marcus Dods. Digireads.com, 2015. Kindle.

———. *The Enchiridion.* Translated by J. F. Shaw. Veritatis, 2012. Kindle.

———. *On the Nature of Good.* Fig Books, 2012. Kindle.

Belcastro, David Joseph. "Voices from the Desert: Merton, Camus and Milosz." In *Merton Annual,* 25:104–12. Louisville: Fons Vitae, 2012.

Bernard, of Clairvaux, Saint. *St. Bernard's Sermons on the Canticle of Canticles.* Dublin: Aeterna, 2014. Kindle.

Camus, Albert. *The Plague.* New York: Vintage, 1991.

Clark, Anthony E. "Can You Trust Thomas Merton?" Catholic.com. May 2008. http://www.catholic.com/magazine/articles/can-you-trust-thomas-merton/.

Coady, Mary Frances. *Merton and Waugh: A Monk, a Crusty Old Man, & the Seven Storey Mountain.* Brewster, MA: Parclete, 2015.

Cooper, David D. *Thomas Merton's Art of Denial: The Evolution of a Radical Humanist.* Athens: University of Georgia Press, 1989.

Dadosky, John D. "Merton's Dialogue with Zen: Pioneering or Passé?" *Fu Jen International Religious Studies* 2.1 (2008) 53–75.

Davis, Stephen T., ed. *Encountering Evil: Live Options in Theodicy.* Atlanta: John Knox, 1981.

———. "Free Will and Evil." In *Encountering Evil: Live Options in Theodicy,* edited by Stephen T. Davis, 73–107. Atlanta: John Knox, 1981.

————. "Introduction." In *Encountering Evil: Live Options in Theodicy*, edited by Stephen T. Davis, vii–xiii. Atlanta: John Knox, 1981.

Fox, Matthew. *A Way to God: Thomas Merton's Creation Spirituality Journey*. Novato, CA: New World Library, 2016.

Gardner, Fiona. *The Only Mind Worth Having: Thomas Merton and the Child Mind*. Eugene, OR: Cascade Books, 2015.

Grayston, Donald. *Thomas Merton and the Noonday Demon: The Camaldoli Correspondence*. Eugene, OR: Cascade Books, 2015.

Griffin, David Ray. "Creation Out of Nothing, Creation Out of Chaos, and the Problem of Evil." In *Encountering Evil: Live Options in Theodicy*, edited by Stephen T. Davis, 108–44. Atlanta: John Knox, 1981.

————. *God, Power, and Evil: A Process Theodicy*. Louisville: Westminster John Knox, 2004.

Griffin, John Howard, and Thomas Merton. *A Hidden Wholeness: The Visual World of Thomas Merton*. Boston: Houghton Mifflin, 1970.

Habito, Ruben L. F. "Hearing the Cries of the World: Thomas Merton's Zen Experience." In *Merton & Buddhism: Wisdom, Emptiness, and Everyday Mind*, edited by Bonnie Bowman Thurston, 91–117. Illustrated by Gray Henry. Fons Vitae Thomas Merton Series. Louisville: Fons Vitae, 2007.

Harvey, B. Peter. *An Introduction to Buddhism: Teachings, History and Practices*. 2nd ed. New York: Cambridge University Press, 2013.

Hick, John. *Evil and the God of Love*. New York: Harper & Row, 1966.

————. "An Irenaean Theodicy." In *Encountering Evil: Live Options in Theodicy*, edited by Stephen T. Davis, 38–72. Atlanta: John Knox, 1981.

Higgins, Michael W. *Thomas Merton: Faithful Visionary*. People of God. Collegeville, MN: Liturgical, 2014.

Hoover, Thomas. *The Zen Experience*. A Plume Book. New York: New American Library, 1980.

Horan, Daniel P., OFM. *The Franciscan Heart of Thomas Merton: A New Look at the Spiritual Inspiration of His Life, Thought, and Writing*. Notre Dame, IN: Ave Maria, 2014.

Inada, Kenneth K. "The Metaphysics of Buddhist Experience and the Whiteheadian Encounter." *Philosophy East and West* 25.4 (1975) 465–88.

Keenan, John P. "The Limits of Thomas Merton's Understanding of Buddhism." In *Merton & Buddhism: Wisdom, Emptiness, and Everyday Mind*, 118–33. Illustrated by Gray Henry. Fons Vitae Thomas Merton Series. Louisville: Fons Vitae, 2007.

Kramp, Joseph M. "Merton's Melancholia: Margie, Monasticism, and the Religion of Hope." *Pastoral Psychology* 55.4 (2007) 441–58.

————. "Merton's Melancholia: Mother, Monasticism, and the Religion of Honor." *Pastoral Psychology* 55.3 (2007) 307–19.

Leclercq, Jean. *The Love of Learning and the Desire for God: A Study of Monastic Culture*. Translated by Catharine Misrahi. New York: Fordham University Press, 1961.

Lipsey, Roger. *Angelic Mistakes: The Art of Thomas Merton*. Boston: New Seeds, 2006.

————. *Make Peace before the Sun Goes Down: The Long Encounter of Thomas Merton and His Abbot, James Fox*. Boston: Shambhala, 2015.

————. "Merton, Suzuki, Zen, Ink: Thomas Merton's Calligraphic Drawings in Context." In *Merton & Buddhism: Wisdom, Emptiness, and Everyday Mind*, edited by Bonnie

BIBLIOGRAPHY

Bowman Thurston, 137–75. Illustrated by Gray Henry. Fons Vitae Thomas Merton Series. Louisville: Fons Vitae, 2007.

Mackie, J. L. "Evil and Omnipotence." *Mind* 64/254 (1955) 200–212.

Merton, Thomas, and Czesław Miłosz. *Striving towards Being: The Letters of Thomas Merton and Czesław Miłosz.* Edited by Robert Faggen. New York: Farrar, Straus & Giroux, 1997.

Merton, Thomas. *The Asian Journal of Thomas Merton.* Edited from his original notebooks by Naomi Burton et al. New York: New Directions, 1975.

————. *Bread in the Wilderness.* New York: New Directions, 1953.

————. "Camus and the Church." In *The Literary Essays of Thomas Merton,* edited by Patrick Hart, 261–74. New York: New Directions, 1981.

————. *Conjectures of a Guilty Bystander.* Garden City, NY: Doubleday, 1966.

————. *The Courage for Truth: The Letters of Thomas Merton to Writers.* Edited by Christine M. Bochen. New York: Farrar, Straus & Giroux, 1993.

————. *Dancing in the Water of Life: Seeking Peace in the Hermitage.* Edited by Robert E. Daggy. Journals of Thomas Merton 5. San Francisco: HarperSanFrancisco, 1997.

————. "The Death of God and the End of History." In *Faith and Violence: Christian Teaching and Christian Practice,* 239–58. Notre Dame, IN: Notre Dame University Press, 1994.

————. *Entering the Silence: Becoming a Monk & Writer.* Edited by Jonathan Montaldo. Journals of Thomas Merton 2. San Francisco: HarperSanFrancisco, 1996.

————. *Exile Ends in Glory: The Life of a Trappistine, Mother M. Berchmans, O.C.S.O.* Milwaukee: Bruce, 1948.

————. *Faith and Violence: Christian Teaching and Christian Practice.* Notre Dame, IN: University of Notre Dame Press, 1968.

————. "Godless Christianity?" In *Faith and Violence: Christian Teaching and Christian Practice,* 259–88. Notre Dame, IN: Notre Dame University Press, 1994.

————. *The Hidden Ground of Love: The Letters of Thomas Merton on Religious Experience and Social Concerns.* Edited by William Henry Shannon. The Thomas Merton Letters Series. New York: Farrar, Straus & Giroux, 1985.

————. *Learning to Love: Exploring Solitude and Freedom.* Edited by Christine M. Bochen. Journals of Thomas Merton 6. San Francisco: HarperSanFrancisco, 1997.

————. *The Life of the Vows: Initiation into the Monastic Tradition 6.* Edited by Patrick F. O'Connell. Monastic Wisdom Series 30. Trappist, KY: Cistercian, 2012.

————. *The Literary Essays of Thomas Merton.* Edited by Patrick Hart. New York: New Directions, 1981.

————. *Love and Living.* Edited by Naomi Burton Stone and Patrick Hart. New York: Farrar, Straus & Giroux, 1979.

————. "The Monk in Diaspora." *New Blackfriars* 45/529–30 (1964) 290–302.

————. *My Argument with the Gestapo: A Macaronic Journal.* Garden City, NY: Doubleday, 1969.

————. *Mystics and Zen Masters.* New York: Farrar, Straus & Giroux, 1967.

————. *The New Man.* New York: Farrar, Straus & Cudahy, 1961.

————. *New Seeds of Contemplation.* Rev. ed. New York: New Directions, 1972.

————. *No Man Is an Island.* New York: Harcourt Brace, 1955.

————. *Opening the Bible.* Collegeville, MN: Liturgical, 1986.

————. *The Other Side of the Mountain: The End of the Journey.* Edited by Patrick Hart. Journals of Thomas Merton 7. San Francisco: HarperSanFrancisco, 1998.

————. *Peace in the Post-Christian Era*. Edited with an introduction by Patricia A. Burton. Maryknoll, NY: Orbis, 2004.

————. *"The Plague* of Albert Camus: A Commentary and Introduction." Edited by Patrick Hart. In *The Literary Essays of Thomas Merton*, 181–217. New York: New Directions, 1981.

————. *President's Death. St. Bernard's Apologia*. Recorded November 23, 1963. CD. Thomas Merton Center at Bellarmine University, Audio and Video Recordings.

————. *The Road to Joy: The Letters of Thomas Merton to New and Old Friends*. Edited by Robert E. Daggy. Thomas Merton Letters Series 2. New York: Farrar, Straus & Giroux, 1989.

————. *Run to the Mountain: The Story of a Vocation*. Edited by Patrick Hart. Journals of Thomas Merton 1. San Francisco: HarperSanFrancisco, 1995.

————. *The School of Charity: The Letters of Thomas Merton on Religious Renewal and Spiritual Direction*. Selected and edited by Patrick Hart. Thomas Merton Letters Series 5. New York: Farrar, Straus & Giroux, 1990.

————. *A Search for Solitude: Pursuing the Monk's True Life*. Edited by Lawrence Cunningham. Journals of Thomas Merton 3. San Francisco: HarperSanFrancisco, 1996.

————. *Seasons of Celebration*. New York: Farrar, Straus & Giroux, 1965.

————. *The Secular Journal of Thomas Merton*. New York: Farrar, Straus & Cudahy, 1959.

————. *Seeds of Contemplation*. Norfolk, CT: New Directions, 1949.

————. *The Seven Storey Mountain*. New York: Harcourt-Brace Jovanovich, 1978.

————. *The Sign of Jonas*. New York: Harcourt, Brace, 1953.

————. "Terror and the Absurd: Violence and Nonviolence in Albert Camus." In *The Literary Essays of Thomas Merton*, edited by Patrick Hart, 232–51. New York: New Directions, 1981.

————. *Thomas Merton in Alaska: Prelude to the Asian Journal; The Alaskan Conferences, Journals, and Letters*. New York: New Directions, 1989.

————. *Turning towards the World (1960–1963): The Pivotal Years*. Edited by Victor A. Kramer. Journals of Thomas Merton 4. San Francisco: HarperSanFrancisco, 1997.

————. "Violence and the Death of God." In *Faith and Violence: Christian Teaching and Christian Practice*, 191–98. Notre Dame, IN: University of Notre Dame Press, 1994.

————. *The Waters of Siloe*. New York: Harcourt Brace, 1949.

————. *What Are These Wounds? The Life of a Cistercian Mystic, Saint Lutgarde of Aywières*. New York: Paulist, 2015.

————. *Witness to Freedom: The Letters of Thomas Merton in Times of Crisis*. Edited by William Henry Shannon. The Thomas Merton Letters Series 5. New York: Farrar, Straus & Giroux, 1994.

————. *Zen and the Birds of Appetite*. New York: New Directions, 1968.

Moses, John. *Divine Discontent: The Prophetic Voice of Thomas Merton*. London: Bloomsbury, 2014.

Mott, Michael. *The Seven Mountains of Thomas Merton*. Boston: Houghton Mifflin, 1984.

Nhất Hạnh, Thich. *The Heart of Understanding: Commentaries on the Prajñaparamita Heart Sutra*. Edited by Peter Levitt. 20th anniversary edition. Berkeley: Parallax, 2009.

————. *The Miracle of Mindfulness: An Introduction to the Practice of Meditation*. Boston: Beacon, 1999.

Niebuhr, Gustav. "Mahanambrata Brahmachari Is Dead at 95." *New York Times*. October 31, 1999. http://www.nytimes.com/1999/11/01/world/mahanambrata-brahmachari-is-dead-at-95.html/.

O'Collins, Gerald, and Edward G. Farrugia. "Theodicy." In *The New Dictionary of Theology*, edited by Joseph A. Komonchak et al., 262. Wilmington, DE: Glazier, 1987.

Ostling, Richard N. "Religion: Merton's Mountainous Legacy." *Time*. December 31, 1984. http://content.time.com/time/subscriber/article/0,33009,951456,00.html/.

Pearson, Paul M. "Beyond the Shadow and Disguise: The Zen Photography of Thomas Merton." In *Merton & Buddhism: Wisdom, Emptiness, and Everyday Mind*, edited by Bonnie Bowman Thurston, 176–97. Illustrated by Gray Henry. Fons Vitae Thomas Merton Series. Louisville: Fons Vitae, 2007.

Plantinga, Alvin. *God, Freedom, and Evil*. 1974. Reprint, Grand Rapids: Eerdmans, 1977.

"Religion: The Mountain." *Time*. April 11, 1949. http://content.time.com/time/magazine/article/0,9171,800091,00.html/.

Rice, Edward. *The Man in the Sycamore Tree: The Good Times and Hard Life of Thomas Merton: An Entertainment with Photographs*. San Diego: Harcourt Brace Jovanovich, 1985.

Samway, Patrick H., SJ, ed. *The Letters of Robert Giroux and Thomas Merton*. Notre Dame: University of Notre Dame Press, 2015.

Scott, Mark S. M. *Pathways in Theodicy: An Introduction to the Problem of Evil*. Minneapolis: Fortress, 2015.

Scruggs, Ryan. "Contemplation and the Cogito: Thomas Merton on the Philosophical Roots of Modern Alienation." In *Merton Annual*, vol. 28, 159–80. Louisville: Fons Vitae, 2015.

Shannon, William H. *Silent Lamp: The Thomas Merton Story*. New York: Crossroad, 1992.

Sharf, Robert H. "The Zen of Japanese Nationalism." *History of Religions* 33/1 (1993) 1–43.

Smith, Huston, and Philip Novak. *Buddhism: A Concise Introduction*. New York: HarperSanFrancisco, 2003.

Suzuki, Daisetz Teitaro. "An Autobiographical Account." In *A Zen Life: D. T. Suzuki Remembered*, edited by Masao Abe, 13–26. New York: Weatherhill, 1986.

———. "Early Memories." In *A Zen Life: D. T. Suzuki Remembered*, edited by Masao Abe, 3–12. New York: Weatherhill, 1986.

———. *Essays in Zen Buddhism (First Series)*. An Evergreen Original New York: Grove Press, 1961.

———. *Essays in Zen Buddhism (Second Series)*. New York: Weiser, 1971.

———. *The Essence of Buddhism*. London: Buddhist Society, 1946.

———. *An Introduction to Zen Buddhism*. Edited by Christmas Humphreys. London: Rider, 1960.

———. *Mysticism: Christian and Buddhist*. World Perspectives 12. New York: Harper, 1957.

———. *Studies in Zen*. Edited by Christmas Humphreys. Mansfield Centre: Martino, 2013.

Thurston, Bonnie Bowman. "The Light Strikes Home: Notes on the Zen Influence in Merton's Poetry." In *Merton & Buddhism: Wisdom, Emptiness, and Everyday Mind*, edited by Bonnie Bowman Thurston, 199–213. Illustrated by Gray Henry. Fons Vitae Thomas Merton Series. Louisville: Fons Vitae, 2007.

———, ed. *Merton & Buddhism: Wisdom, Emptiness, and Everyday Mind*. Illustrated by Gray Henry. Fons Vitae Thomas Merton Series. Louisville: Fons Vitae, 2007.

Whitehead, Alfred North. *Process and Reality: An Essay in Cosmology: Corrected Edition.* Edited by David Ray Griffin and Donald W. Sherburne. New York: Free Press, 1978. Kindle.

Wilhelm, Gundert. "A Sower of Seeds." In *A Zen Life: D. T. Suzuki Remembered*, edited by Masao Abe, 136–42. New York: Weatherhill, 1986.

Wilkes, Paul, ed. *Merton, by Those Who Knew Him Best.* San Francisco: Harper & Row, 1984.

Zhuangzi, and Thomas Merton. *The Way of Chuang-Tzŭ.* New York: New Directions, 1965.

Name/Subject Index